PEER PRESSURE REVERSAL

An Adult Guide to Developing a Responsible Child

Second Edition

Sharon Scott, L.P.C., L.M.F.T.

Illustrated by Steve Wilda

HRD Press, Inc.
Amherst, Massachusetts

ISBN 0-87425-408-6

Published by **HRD Press, Inc.**
22 Amherst Road
Amherst, MA 01002
(800) 822-2801 (US and Canada)
(413) 253-3490 (FAX)
http://www.hrdpress.com (Internet)

Composition by Page Design Services
Editorial Services by Mary George
Cover Design by Eileen Klockars

 PRINTED IN CANADA

WITH LOVE AND APPRECIATION . . .
to my parents, Johnny and Harry V. Scott, Jr.,
my late grandparents, Audrey and Harry V. Scott, Sr.,
and Maggie and Robert Smith Nicholson, Sr.,
who, by their example, taught me good, basic values
and an appreciation for life.

TABLE OF CONTENTS

Preface ix
Foreword xiii

1. NEGATIVE PEER PRESSURE: Introduction
   and Overview 1

2. PEER PRESSURE REVERSAL (PPR): An Essential
   Skill to Give a Child 29
   PPR Step 1: Check Out the Scene 34
   PPR Step 2: Make a Good Decision 44
   PPR Step 3: Act to Avoid Trouble 51
   PPR in Action 76

3. TEACHING PPR: How a Parent Can
   Deliver the Skill 85
   Teaching Step 1: Schedule 88
   Teaching Step 2: Introduce 90
   Teaching Step 3: Discuss 94
   Teaching Step 4: Practice 100
   Teaching Step 5: Feedback 102
   Teaching PPR: Lights, Camera, Action 106

4. TEACHING PPR: Teaching Delivery for
   the Classroom 113
   PPR Lesson Plan 116
   I: Introduction 116
   II: Present 120
   III: Exercise 120
   IV: Summary 124
   V: Follow-Up Ideas 124

5. REINFORCING PPR: Maintaining Responsible
   Behavior and Emphasizing the Positive 127
   Reinforcing Technique 1:
      Encouraging the Positive 131

Reinforcing Technique 2:
    Disciplining Effectively 149
Reinforcing Technique 3:
    Using Organized Activity to Dilute Peer Pressure ... 168
Reinforcing Technique 4:
    Influencing the Child's Choice of Friends 187
Reinforcing Technique 5:
    Taking Advantage of Multi-Parental Networking 201
Special Note about Drugs 216

6. PEER PRESSURE REVERSAL: Summary 223

RESOURCES 227

ABOUT THE AUTHOR 235

PREFACE

As a parent, educator, or other professional helper working with youth, no doubt you have seen the amount of negative pressure that young people can and do exert on one another. Even though I have been counseling and training youth since 1970, I am still alarmed at the effect their peers have on them and how modern-day peer pressure becomes stronger each year.

The soaring rate of juvenile crime, the widespread use of drugs, the rising school dropout rate, and the alarming increase in teenage pregnancies and adolescent suicides attest to our society's failure to provide its youth with sufficient skills to develop into capable, healthy human beings. The seven years that I worked with the First Offender Program at the Dallas Police Department broadened my awareness of how "good kids" from caring, loving homes can make poor decisions that result in broken laws and shocked parents. The single major factor influencing those poor decisions was negative peer pressure. And so often such crimes were committed out of boredom, or on a dare or challenge!

Children are growing up faster than ever before. The difficult decisions that were once made in the late teens (or early 20s) are today being made by children in elementary school. Parents teach their children right from wrong and hope this will automatically prepare them to make good decisions. Not so, as most kids lack the expertise and quick responses required in peer pressure situations. I constantly talk with parents who complain about the negative peer pressure encountered by their child. They see the problem as the poor quality of friends in their child's school or neighborhood. The *real* problem is their child's lack of confidence and expertise in decision making! Parents who have children in public school sometimes want to enroll them in private school. Parents may even consider moving to a "better" neighborhood to get their child away from the negative influence of peers, not realizing that peer pressure situations abound everywhere.

Television tends to reflect our society's values. When we were growing up, families watched shows like *Father Knows Best, The Adventures of Ozzie and Harriet,* and *Leave It to Beaver,* which provided role models of the healthy family. Kids watched shows like *Lassie, Roy Rogers,* and *Walt Disney's Wonderful World of Color,* which modeled positive activities and showed the "good guys in the white hats" winning. Today there are few replacements perpetuating these examples.

This book is not written in the terminology of concept and theory. Rather, it presents Peer Pressure Reversal to adults in a skills-based, step-by-step approach that can be immediately applied to teaching and training children and teens. I have used this approach in one-on-one counseling situations and group training classes, as well as on a school district-wide basis. I have taught these skills as a preventive technique and also as an intervention approach to youth actively involved in negative peer pressure. You can too! We can work together to produce responsible citizens by preparing young people to think and act on their own. We *must* do this to ensure their real growth as individuals.

The second edition of *Peer Pressure Reversal* contains much updated information and additional features and suggestions. It presents ways that parents and educators can try to counter the negative societal changes that make children grow up too fast, as well as a method for teaching simplified Peer Pressure Reversal to children as young as age five. There is also a new chapter designed to help professionals outline their teaching delivery of PPR.

This edition could not have been completed without the assistance of Michelle Perkus, my typist, and the cooperation of HRD Press staff including my fabulous editor, Mary George, my cover designer, Eileen Klockars, and marketing assistance from Linda Reese and Martha Cantwell. I would also like to extend my gratitude once again to the people whose work on the first edition contributed to its success, Aleen Sullivan, Clare Miller, Peggy Miller, and the entire staff at HRD Press.

I owe a special debt of gratitude to Dr. Robert Carkhuff, Dr. Tom Collingwood, and Dr. Bernard Berenson, whose influence on my professional life has been deep and lasting.

Finally, I would like to express my appreciation to all the young people, parents, counselors, and teachers who have supported my work. Thanks for buying the first edition and writing to me about your success with it. Thanks also to the universities that use this as a text in their counseling and education departments. We must impart specific skills—not vague theory—if we expect to help kids grow up safely in this overly sophisticated world in which they live.

— Sharon Scott

Dallas, Texas

FOREWORD

by Robert R. Carkhuff, Ph.D.
Author, *The Art of Helping*

As information explodes upon us, the relationships between parent and child become more problematic. Each succeeding wave of information yields a wave of youth subcultures uniquely impacted by the interaction of forces—the possibility of nuclear catastrophe, the job market and the economy, the independence of educational achievement and life achievement, the family and sexual mores. The data base changes for each succeeding generation, and with these changes the generations themselves change. Adolescents look quizzically at adults who have not processed the information that young people must address on a daily basis. They question the adult values that were born of a different age, a slower time, a calmer time. The peer pressures become inordinate.

Not all of the peer pressures are destructive. Many provide the joy of living—relating to each other, discovering and creating their own culture—its music, dress, language, and other customs. Other peer pressures are clearly destructive. They precipitate the crises, the catastrophes, the tragedies of living—the pressures to drink and do other drugs, to share sexual favors prematurely, to be intolerant of the traditional values of the older generation, thus distancing themselves and not benefiting from the guidance of those who truly love them.

Sharon Scott has worked long and hard at reversing this peer pressure. *Peer Pressure Reversal* is a culmination of her efforts. It provides guidance to parents, teachers, and concerned community citizens to enable them to provide the PPR skills to children. It emphasizes the following steps:

1. Teaching PPR, which includes the skills of Checking Out the Scene, Making a Good Decision, and Acting to Avoid Trouble, and

2. Reinforcing PPR by Encouraging the Positive, Disciplining Effectively, Using Organized Activity to Dilute Peer Pressure, Influencing the Child's Choice of Friends, and Taking Advantage of Multi-Parental Networking.

These principles are concisely developed, anecdotally illustrated, and programmatically effective.

Ms. Scott's credentials include directing the now-famous First Offender Program of the Dallas Police Department. Originally created by Dr. Tom Collingwood, this diversion program reduced delinquency from a base rate of 64 percent to a diversion rate of 21 percent for 10,000 young people. This was done by teaching the parents and young people the skills they needed to live effectively with each other and in their worlds. Ms. Scott has called upon her invaluable experience in developing and demonstrating her PPR principles. It is a real contribution to the beleaguered parent and conflicted youth in a time of great need for all of us.

1. NEGATIVE PEER PRESSURE:

Introduction and Overview

"What's different about the peer pressure confronting today's young people, and how can I help my child?"

Every day your child is pressured by his or her peers to think as they think and to do as they do. As a concerned adult, you probably have questions about negative peer influence.

How can you help your child to withstand negative peer pressure and still be popular . . . to "mainstream" without losing his or her values . . . to stay out of trouble . . . to get along with others but be able to say "no" when needed? You were faced with these challenges as a young person, but the pressures then were not as sophisticated and intense as they are now.

The changes in our way of life and society during the past 20 to 30 years challenge both children and parents. These changes subtly encourage children to grow up faster and force them to make difficult, often adult decisions at earlier ages. These pressures can range from talking in class to staying out past a curfew to experimenting with drugs and sex.

The situation has worsened since Lance Morrow wrote these eloquent words in *Time,* August 8, 1988:

> It is both the best and the worst times for children. Their world contains powers and perspectives inconceivable to a child 50 years ago: computers; longer life expectancy; the entire planet accessible through television, satellites, air travel. But so much knowledge and choices can be chaotic and dangerous. School curricula have been adapted to teach about new topics: AIDS, adolescent suicide, drug and alcohol abuse, incest. Trust is the child's natural inclination, but the world has become untrustworthy. The hazards of the adult world, its sometimes fatal temptations, descend upon children so easily that the ideal of childhood is demoralized.

3

Children aren't born knowing how to handle modern-day peer pressure, nor do parents and other adults automatically know how to help them. This book will help you teach this skill to your child (or student or client) by using a simple, practical, and proven-effective formula: Peer Pressure Reversal, or PPR. In the process, you will also help your child develop into a more responsible, happy "winner."

Understanding Peer Pressure: Stories and Statistics

Before you discover the PPR skill and how to deliver it to your child, it may be helpful for you to "experience" for a few moments the weight of peer pressure as it exists today.

The following examples of negative peer pressure and its results are disturbing. The tendency is to assume that your child will never be exposed to such pressures and that your child will not succumb to them even if he or she is exposed. These true stories are about everyday children and problematic situations that your child could encounter. Any experienced youth counselor can confirm that negative peer pressure is extremely common to all levels of society. No social stratum is immune to peer pressure or to the poor decision making and pain that so often result from it.

These stories not only demonstrate why it is vital that children be equipped with the PPR skill, but also underscore why adults must learn to be aware of, and protect children from, the extreme pressures and dangers facing today's youth. Now, let's take a look at these stories.

- There was a group of third graders who would walk home together from school every day. The route involved crossing a busy street. After a while, the children began taunting one another to take a shortcut across this street instead of "acting like babies" and using the crosswalk. As time passed, more and more children were taking the shortcut, avoiding the crosswalk because they didn't want to be teased. As you have probably guessed, the ultimate outcome was tragic. One child was struck by a car and suffered serious injury.

- A bright sixth-grade student dreamed of having a career as an astronaut. Because of his intelligence, disciplined personality, and favorite hobbies (including model-rocket building), his chances were good that one day he would fulfill his dream.

His high standards and search for excellence made him stand out at school, as did his eagerness to please his teacher. At the teacher's call, he would run to be the first in line, and soon his classmates began making fun of him. They noticed that he liked to cooperate with adults and to succeed. Many of the kids who preferred to goof off started calling him a "goody-goody" and teased him about being teacher's pet and being smart.

He had no tools that would help him deal with this peer pressure, and the situation was threatening his natural need to be liked. Because he needed peer approval more than his achievement goal, he began to deal with the problem in the only way he knew how: by conforming in performance and behavior. He started intentionally missing questions on tests so that he scored in the low 90s instead of his usual high 90s. He stopped running to the teacher's call, and began holding back so that he would be fifth or sixth in line instead of first.

This child stopped pushing himself to fulfill his potential. He lowered his standards and reduced his possibility of meeting his goal, which he had once wanted badly to achieve. He became depressed and confused, because he was being offered an impossible choice between reaching his personal goals and achieving peer approval by fitting in.

- Our next story focuses on an attractive 15-year-old girl. Her father was a professional in the community, and the family had a good standard of living. The girl had an older sister who seemed to have everything going for her: she made extremely high grades, was talented musically, and had a lot of friends. The 15-year-old felt hopeless about ever achieving the standards set by her older sister, and this made her feel like a disappointment and a failure.

Deeply discouraged, she started hanging around some of the poorly adjusted kids at school, with whom she did not feel inferior. Exposed to their peer pressure, and little inclined to resist it, she became more and more influenced by their behavior and prompting. Before long, the course of her life was in a downward spiral. It started with skipping a school class now and then, and led to occasional drinking on weekends. That developed into marijuana use and to sneaking out of the house at night to see a boyfriend who was not acceptable to the family.

When her parents tried to control the many problems that had developed, the girl ran away from home. She was picked up by the police but continued sneaking out at night, and ultimately ended up pregnant and seeking an abortion.

- Although the next dare is an old one, it was traumatic for the child, his parents, and the very worried elementary school principal on whose snow-packed playground it took place. One second-grader dared friends to stick their tongues to a metal pole. One boy accepted the dare, and when he pulled away from the frozen pole, most of the skin was torn from his tongue and lips. A hospital visit and months of speech therapy followed this dangerous prank.

- A seventh-grade boy was invited to a party. The parents of the hosting child were at home; however, they stayed out of sight the whole time and soon were forgotten. The kids started playing "Spin the Bottle." Someone got a bottle of alcohol out of the parents' liquor cabinet and shared it with the others.

This dangerous turn of events resulted in a situation that was far from "fun and games" for the boy. He was approached by a girl who, having "won" him on a spin of the bottle, wanted him to go with her to a vacant bedroom. He went, because of the peer pressure, although he was still at an age where he was more interested in football than girls. Under intense pressure, at first he felt trapped into undressing with the girl, but then he thought of an excuse: that he believed he heard the parents in a nearby room. The two children rushed out of the bedroom, and so the boy's problem was resolved before it got completely out of hand; however, he had still been through a disturbing experience. A child who can't think that quickly, or for whom there's no obvious excuse at hand, might not have scraped through the ordeal as well as this boy did.

Widespread sexual experimentation by both genders is starting younger in this society. According to the National Academy of Science, 67 percent of females and 80 percent of males are sexually active before they leave their teens. Either boys or girls may find themselves confronted by sexual peer pressure, and they need a skillful way to protect themselves in such situations and to delay sexual experience until they are more mature and preferably married.

- This story involves a 13-year-old girl whose family moved to a new town one summer. School started, and she kept her usual good study habits, maintaining A's and B's. But in her efforts to make friends quickly and fit into the new social scene, she became involved in some peer pressure situations that she would have resisted had she been in her hometown and on familiar, established ground.

It was not long before her misconduct extended beyond the classroom. After school, when her parents were still at work, she would spend all her time talking on the phone with her new friends, instead of doing her chores and homework. Her grades began to suffer. When her friends discovered that her parents were not home in the afternoon, they started showing up at her house, bringing along beer to share. Because of the pressure to fit in, the girl allowed this.

Soon she was not even going home after school, but to places like shopping centers, where she and her friends could "hang out." The ultimate outcome? She and her friends were caught shoplifting.

- Our final story involves an 18-year-old high school senior from a prominent family. Unsure about where he would attend college, he decided to visit several Ivy League campuses to see what they were like. During one visit, an attractive 21-year-old "tour guide," herself a student at the university, offered him marijuana and then proceeded to have sex with him. Later, he felt embarrassed over how she had manipulated him; moreover, he was terrified that he had contracted some disease from her.

In addition to these troubling peer-pressure stories are the disastrous situations we too often hear about on the national news. In New Jersey, a group of young people, all from affluent backgrounds, takes advantage of a mildly retarded 17-year-old girl, abusing and raping her. In Texas, 12 high school seniors from middle-class, church-going families are sentenced to prison for the armed robbery of 20 fast-food restaurants. Prior to their arrests, several of these boys were awarded athletic scholarships! And in Ohio, two seventh-grade students are charged with plotting to kill a teacher. Their classmates had bet nearly $200 on whether the two would carry out their plans. One girl later explains that she had no choice in the matter because the other kids put her on the spot.

Children all over the nation have become involved in self-destructive, and even criminal, activity because they don't feel competent enough to make good decisions. Trouble often results when they can't say no. Often they don't believe something bad will happen to them, and many simply don't know how to manage peer pressure situations that get out of control.

We all have to make many decisions every day—choices that range from the simple to the complex. A percentage of those decisions are poor ones, on every level of society and in any age group. And this percentage will rise as the pressures become more and more difficult to handle.

Despite the intensifying pressure, you may be a parent who feels confident of your child's decision-making capability and moral strength (i.e., ability to recognize negative consequences). However, decision making and perceptiveness are only part of successfully reversing peer pressure: the other part is action!

Modern-day pressures can overwhelm the child who has not been *trained to take action* to prevent trouble or avoid it. The moral child may be able to tell right from wrong and to think through a situation, figuring out its potential outcomes. Yet, without training in the "how to's" of peer pressure reversal, that child will enter society only half-equipped to deal with the pressures that he or she is likely to encounter.

We thus need to do more than help our children develop conscience and forethought; we must also teach them action-oriented skills—ways to bridge inner knowledge and outer demands. Otherwise, our children will be at a strict disadvantage in peer pressure situations and come away from them burdened with feelings of failure and guilt.

The hard fact is, when confronted by the serious, adult-level choices so prevalent in the youth culture of today, many children are choosing poorly. The statistics on rising youth substance abuse, youth involvement in crime, teenage pregnancy, and adolescent suicide all point to one conclusion: young people lack the skills they need to manage their lives well through sound, mature decision making and positive action. To realize the problems that youth are facing today, consider the statistics* below:

- One in 10 teenage girls (one million) get pregnant each year.
- The suicide rate for teens has doubled since 1968.
- Teenage arrests are up thirtyfold since 1950.
- Homicide is the leading cause of death among 15- to 19-year-old minority youth.
- On average, sexually active 17- to 19-year-old urban males claim to have had six partners.

Sources: Alan Guttmacher Institute, National Association of State Boards of Education, American Medical Association, National Center for Disease Control, 1992 FBI Annual Crime Report, University of Michigan National Institute for Drug Abuse, 1995 PRIDE National Drug Survey.

- During 1995, 28.1 percent of junior high teens smoked cigarettes, with 44 percent of senior high students admitting to smoking.

- Thirty-two percent of eighth graders reported riding in a car in the last month with someone who was drinking or using other drugs.

- Marijuana use among sixth through eighth graders increased from 4.5 percent to 9.5 percent from 1990 to 1995, and from 16.9 percent to 28.2 percent among high school students; inhalants also increased significantly among sixth through twelfth graders from 1990 to 1995; LSD use is once again on the increase.

- Ninety-two percent of high school seniors have had experience with alcohol, with 66 percent being current users (i.e., used in the past 30 days) and 37.5 percent reporting at least one occasion of heavy drinking in the past two weeks (i.e., five or more drinks in a row).

- Violent crimes among juveniles increased 23.7 percent in the past decade (among white teens the increase was 44 percent; among black teens the increase was 19 percent; other races dropped 53 percent).

These statistics make clear just how deeply our society's youth need help and guidance.

Childhood and Today's Lifestyle: The Problems Facing Us

Fortunately, children *can* be taught how to make decisions that are compatible with family values and how to take action to reverse negative peer pressure; but they need adults to teach them these skills, and there are many obstacles to success. Foremost among them is our high-tech lifestyle, which continually increases the negative messages and invitations that it sends to children while reducing the quality of adult interaction with children. These messages are often conveyed or reinforced by the popular media, which, along with the state of family life today, present us with a number of serious problems.

Media-Related Problems

More images are communicated to the masses than ever before. Many of those images are too adult for children and conflict with family values. The weight of approval is given, either overtly or subtly, to social dangers such as alcohol and other drug use, violence, dishonesty, selfishness, biased and merely physical standards of beauty, and unhealthy sexuality. Children receive these messages from the many technetronic and traditional forms of the media: television, videos, movies, radio, live entertainment, magazines, books, and advertisements.

From the media, children learn more at earlier ages, and of course imitate what they see. The media also reinforce peer pressure: if you want to have a good personality and be popular, you have to wear a certain brand of jeans or use a particular toothpaste, for instance, or else you won't be a part of the "in" group. This puts a lot of pressure on parents who are trying to raise their children according to sound values.

Television, one of the powerful forces influencing people's behavior today, tends to undermine, rather than to support, the institution of the family. On many situation comedies, sarcastic parents and children are the norm. As a result, real-life parents who are concerned about their children are forced to worry about the effects of such programming. Does Bart Simpson encourage underachieving? Will a child exposed to MTV's *Beavis and Butt-head* copy the sociopathic behaviors (e.g., fire setting and animal cruelty) exhibited on that show? And direct parental supervision can only go so far: what is forbidden at home may be available on videotape at a friend's house.

Research has shown that concerns regarding televised content are not unfounded. The Center for Population Options reports that in an average year of television viewing, the typical teenager is bombarded with more than 14,000 scenes of implied sexual intercourse, comment, or innuendo. The National Coalition on Television Violence found that first-run syndicated cartoons average 37 violent acts per hour! On average, a child who has just completed *elementary* school has viewed 8,000 murders and 100,000 violent acts on television, according to the American Psychological Association. And we wonder why we have children carrying weapons to school!

Daytime talk shows (many of which are aired after school) often highlight the misfits of society, "normalizing" topics that only a small percent of our society deals with. Tabloid television shows crowd programming schedules, offering little more than sensationalism and a distortion of fact. Even the "real-life" crime shows tend to fall into this camp. I know a man who requires his children to watch these crime shows so that they will learn to be careful. My opinion is that the sensational, negative aspects of those shows would make anyone—children and adults alike—skeptical, critical, and scared. There are healthier ways to teach our children about personal safety issues.

The American Psychological Association states that nearly 40 years of accumulated research on the impact of television violence demonstrates a correlation between viewing violence and aggressive behavior. Leonard Eron, Ph.D., a professor of psychology at the University of Michigan's Institute for Social Research, conducted a 22-year longitudinal study on the effects of television viewing. His subjects, who lived in semi-rural New York, were examined at ages 8, 19, and 30. He discovered that those who watched the most television violence at age 8 later inflicted harsher punishment on their own children and acted more aggressively when drinking; they also were convicted of more serious crimes by age 30. Another 25-year study, by Ron Sloby, Ph.D., senior scientist at Education Development Center, Newton, Massachusetts, documented four negative effects on children as a result of viewing television and film violence:

1. "Aggressor effect"—often demonstrated by boys who identify with violent male heroes and are more likely to behave aggressively

2. "Victim effect"—evident in girls who identify with female victims in shows and are more fearful, mistrustful, and self-protective

3. "Bystander effect"—seen in increased callousness, apathy, and emotional desensitization toward violence

4. "Appetite effect"—seen in the heightened desire to view more violence and engage in violent behaviors, including joining a gang or carrying weapons

(For more information about this study, see *America's Smallest School: The Family,* a publication prepared in 1992 by the Educational Testing Service, New Jersey.)

According to *Education Extra,* from 1982 to 1990 the number of young people watching more than three hours of television per day doubled—for 13-year-olds the figure rose to 70 percent. Among 9-year-olds, almost one-fourth were watching more than six hours per day. If this trend is not reversed, the source of most kids' values will be their peers and the media—for better or for worse!

Family-Related Problems

Our children have been put in a precarious position: not only are they continuously bombarded with outside messages and opportunities beyond our control, but in many cases they are insufficiently reinforced in the home to withstand negative pressures. Isolation and lack of time for family communication, family work, and family play is at an all-time high. A 1991 Louis Harris survey showed that the amount of leisure time enjoyed by the average American had declined by 37 percent since 1973, while the average work week had increased from less than 41 hours to nearly 47 hours. Many consider absence from the home a new form of neglect.

Latchkey children are home alone after school to fend for themselves or to supervise younger children. For the first time, according to a report by the Center for the Study of Social Policy, the majority of women with children under age 6 are working—60 percent as compared to 46 percent in 1980. Most of these children are in day care. Non-family adults or children are rearing the little ones—again, for better or for worse.

Our way of life, with its lack of leisure time and abundance of stress, does little to compensate families for their lost sense of solidarity and increasing fragmentation. At best, people make a paycheck large enough for them to crowd their homes with labor-saving devices and electronic sources of entertainment, many of which simply contribute to the problem. Those labor-saving devices "save" family members from working together on a task and talking with one another; those sources of entertainment lend enjoyment in almost any form but family communication and interaction.

For example, consider once again that virtual necessity, the television. It has been dubbed "the global hearth," yet within many households this "hearth" does more to isolate family members than unify them. It often supplants communication and provides only a passive form of shared recreation. Moreover, few families have only one television, as most did years ago, which makes matters worse. At least during the early years of this medium, in the 1950s, the family sat in the same room and shared something that was fun and new, watching shows that emphasized family values. And video rentals, if not monitored, can bring more sex and violence into the home.

Certainly the families of the past also had obstacles to overcome, and I am not advocating a return to the Dark Ages. But we need to be conscious of how our interactions in living, working, and playing are diminishing. At one time, for instance, dinner was the primary time for family communication; now family members tend to "graze" in shifts. When the only phone in the house was the kitchen phone, parents could hear what was going on in their child's world; today homes are equipped with multiple phones, at least one behind a door that tightly closes. Teenagers used to be less mobile, and parents had a better chance to monitor their activities; now many teenagers have cars, and parents have less control over them.

The "freedoms" that we have gained in recent years, and the technology that we invest in and support, may afford us some means of saving time. But if that time is not put back into parenting and family interaction, it is wasted at the expense of our children's wholeness and health. Parents need to review the reasons why time has become such an issue in their lives: perhaps if they spent less time working for external success and a higher standard of living, they would have enough of this priceless commodity to focus their efforts on developing responsible children.

One of the most essential elements of this development is communication. And today what communication a family does have tends to be of poor quality. The most common interaction at home often bears the anxious or sour tone of fussing, nagging, and lecturing. This poor communication is a result of parents having little time for doing more than keeping order—a situation in which it's easy to notice the negative while taking the good for granted.

For example, here are some typical remarks that a teenager hears from a parent during the course of a Saturday.

—"You gonna sleep all day?"

—"Who told you to use my hair dryer?"

—"Turn down the TV."

—"Clean up your dishes from the table."

—"You made your bed yet?"

—"Why don't you iron it yourself?"

—"Somebody has to go to the store for_____."

—"Haven't you done your homework yet?"

—"Your shirt's sticking out" . . . and so on.

This kind of communication isn't worth much to either the child or the parent-child relationship. To improve the situation, we must acquire parenting skills that emphasize positive, effective communication—skills that *reduce* nagging and *produce* results.

In many ways, children need their parents' help and support more than ever. And in many ways, parents have to be stronger and more resourceful than ever if they are to fulfill that need. Why? Because today's lifestyle has weakened their, and their children's, traditional support-system—the combined forces of the extended family and the immediate community—while nearly redefining the family structure and homelife.

A Harvard University study found that in the 1950s, 60 percent of U.S. families with children were headed by a biological father who worked out of the home and a biological mother who stayed at home (and worked there!). Today, less than 11 percent fall into that category. That such a change has taken place as divorce rates have soared and single-parent households have proliferated is no small coincidence. The financial pressures that beset intact families are simply multiplied in these instances, especially for custodial parents. According to the 1986 U.S. Census Bureau, within four months of a divorce, the parent who keeps the children suffers, on average, a 37 percent decline in his or her income. In turn, the difficulties of parenting—including providing children with the support they need to combat negative peer pressure—are multiplied too.

It is worth remembering that, at one time, parents were not the only adults who acted as caretakers and role models for children. Grandparents, aunts, and uncles were on hand, lending their assistance via the network of the extended family. Neighbors were a notable presence as well, forming an essential part of the surrounding community. This was generally good for children and parents alike. With extra adults around, children are apt to receive an additional helping of attention and guidance, which encourages them to develop responsible behavior and a good self-image, while parents receive support for their parallel efforts.

Today, the extended family is on the "endangered species" list and fast becoming extinct. For any number of reasons—mobility and job relocation among them—relatives now often live at great distances from one another. Combined with the rise of single-parent families, this means that the remaining parent is the only adult with whom many children have a close relationship.

The once-supportive neighborhood network has also changed. Often we have no friendships with our neighbors, even those immediately around us. We used to know the whole neighborhood block and could readily see what was going on from our front porches and through our chainlink fences. Now our small families build high, wooden fences around their backyards, and front porches are practically a relic of days gone by.

Traditionally, neighbors (and relatives as well) joined forces, working to guard children from danger by establishing, and drawing on, community spirit. The community emphasized good social values and exerted healthy pressure on everyone to abide by them; anyone who resisted did so at the risk of social ostracism. If another parent saw something inappropriate happening and your child was involved, that parent wouldn't hesitate to call you, and you would appreciate that call and immediately take some action to remedy the harmful situation. And if a child got in trouble at school, then that child got in trouble later on at home. All adults who knew the community's children were involved in the upbringing of those children. Did this form of adult supervision make a difference in our communities? For an answer, take a look at the following information from California's Fullerton Police Department and the California Department of Education.

Top Seven School Problems	
1940s	1990s
1. Talking in class	1. Drug use
2. Chewing gum	2. Alcohol use
3. Making noise	3. Pregnancy
4. Running in halls	4. Suicide
5. Cutting in line	5. Rape
6. Dress code violations	6. Robbery
7. Littering	7. Assault

Unfortunately, today if we call a child's parents and report something amiss concerning the child, the parents may become defensive, even hostile, and tell us "not *my* child." They may completely refuse to listen to our efforts to unify as parents. Sometimes, merely because we don't know the parent well, we hesitate to call and give information. The theme of many neighborhoods is "mind your own business." So our children are often out there without adult supervision.

As if this lack of guidance, the imbalances in our lifestyle, and a host of other problems have not given us enough to worry about, we must also be especially diligent so that our children do not catch "affluenza." It is also called "I want" and often means "I get." Not all children are taught the direct relationship between effort and reward. They see their friends with certain brands of clothes that commercials claim will make them desirable, and with tricycles, bicycles, or cars that supposedly will make them popular, and they begin the standard chant: "I want one, too!" Many children get allowances as a basic birthright, for there is no link between money and home or school responsibilities. When children are overindulged, it may have an effect even later in life. When adult children cannot continue the lifestyle to which their parents have accustomed them, many move back home. A 1987 study by Brown University found that the number of single 20- to 24-year-old men and women living with parents had increased about 25 percent since 1974. In the 25 to 29 age bracket, the increase was more than 60 percent.

All of these changes in society converge to leave children unprecedentedly vulnerable to public pressure, especially peer pressure, which is so close to "home" and which is often substituted for family influence. A gang is a perfect example of a substitute family.

Giving Childhood Back to Children: Some Suggestions

So what can be done to help counter the negative societal effects on children? Following are two lists—one for parents and one for educators and other professionals—that offer some tips on how to give children back their childhood and help them cope with the changes and pressures of society that encourage them to grow up too fast.

How Parents Can Help Alleviate Societal Pressures

1. Manage your own peer pressure. Avoid letting the latest trend ("what's in") rule your buying habits. Don't overschedule yourself because you cannot turn someone down. If other parents are letting their children go places or do things that you don't think your children are ready for, don't compromise your point of view. The bottom line is, if you cannot say no when you need to, how do you expect your children to say no when they need to?

2. Get to know some of your neighbors. Welcome new neighbors by taking a baked item over to their house. Sponsor a block party. Ask for Neighborhood Watch through your local police department. If a neighbor reports to you about your child's misbehavior, thank him or her.

3. Attend PTA/PTO, with the expressed purpose of meeting other parents in your community. Sit next to someone whom you don't know and introduce yourself.

4. If grandparents live afar, try to stay in touch through letters (with pictures), telephone calls, or even cassette tapes.

5. Adopt a senior citizen in your community or local nursing home as a substitute grandparent. Ask the nursing home's activity director for the name of a resident who has few visitors and may need a friend.

6. If your child spends weekends at the other parent's home, attempt to work with your former spouse on establishing similar rules and chores for the child. That way your child will know what is expected of him or her and feel more secure.

7. Monitor television! There are many options to choose from, including a no-television night when everyone participates in a family activity, or a DEAR (Drop Everything And Read) night. Some parents allow their child to watch as many hours of television at night as the child spent studying and reading that day after school. Other parents do not allow any television on school nights.

When viewing television with children, make fun of the commercials that attempt to link our self-esteem with what toothpaste we use or brand of blue jeans we wear. Or hit the mute button on your remote control when a commercial comes on. Don't use television as a babysitter, as the number of hours watched by most children should be reduced. Do watch good family, nature, or cultural programs with your family, and discuss them later on. Avoid letting children watch programming that encourages sarcastic communication or portrays unhealthy sexuality and violence. Teach your children to critique what they watch. Some parents allow after-school viewing but turn off the set in the evening, when the family is most likely to gather together.

8. Make mealtimes (breakfast or dinner) a time for casual chitchat ("What did you do today?"), news tidbits ("Did you read about . . . ?"), or other general topics. This is also a time when children can hear about your day and actually learn more about the real world. And, of course, no television or telephone interruptions should be allowed.

9. Don't put a telephone or television in your child's room unless you want to (a) see your child less often, and (b) argue more when you do see him or her!

10. Select healthy role models from among your peers and community speakers, and introduce your children to them. You might even consider taking your children to work with you one day. A 1991 study, conducted by the American Association of University Women, concluded that both boys and girls suffer from low self-esteem during adolescence. As girls emerge from adolescence, however, their self-worth is markedly lower. This is a time when many girls look to a boyfriend, in inappropriate sexual ways, in an attempt to boost their view of themselves. Both boys and girls need lots of positive attention from parents, other adults such as coaches and youth ministers, and even mentors from possible career choices.

11. Educate your children on the harmful effects of tobacco, alcohol, and other drugs. Information is available in maga-

zines and free pamphlets from some of your social service agencies.

12. Practice what you preach. If you drink, never drink and drive (many teens complain to me that after they are through with a babysitting job, a parent who has been drinking drives them home). If you are single, it will be confusing for your child if you bring a date home to spend the night. If you have a "fuzzbuster" (radar detector) in your car, you are giving your child the message that it is okay to break a law (speed), just as long as you don't get caught. Most of us don't like to look at our own behaviors, but children look at them, and base their behaviors more on what they see rather than on what they hear.

Add some of your own ideas about how you can tone down negative societal effects on your child:

✍

✍

✍

✍

✍

✍

✍

✍

How Teachers Can Help Alleviate Societal Pressures

1. Make your classroom a place where students learn the value of community. A third-grade teacher from a Detroit inner-city school, Howe Elementary, told me how she and other teachers were working to provide a safe learning environment for their students. She also described her efforts to make her student group feel, and conduct itself, like a close-knit community. These efforts include using imagination and a few props to transform the classroom into a small town. Each row of desks becomes a street, and the students select its name. One corner of the classroom is filled with plants and becomes the town park (useful if someone needs a time-out). Another corner is filled with books and becomes the library, and reading for fun is encouraged. Being responsible and caring for the town is encouraged too, including picking up any trash on the floor, even if someone else dropped it there.

2. Know your students' names and stand at your classroom door to greet each one as they enter your class. This makes them feel special and shows that you are friendly and care about them.

3. Do something unusual every now and then, so no one will want to miss your class. Ideas include dressing in a costume of a time period you are studying, or bringing to class an old book on the subject you are teaching.

4. Boost the self-esteem of your students. I have seen signs in some classrooms or principals' offices that read, "The Most Important Person in This School." When you stand in front of the sign, you are looking into a mirror!

5. During a visit to P.T. Young Middle School in Marshall, Texas, I noticed an interesting display in the front hallway. Hundreds of comets had been cut from yellow construction paper and taped to the wall. The display was titled "Honesty Board." Each comet bore a note of recognition for an honest act, such as "Suzy Jones found $1.00 in the cafeteria and turned it in to the office on April 20th."

6. Emphasize the importance of working on problems rather than merely complaining about them, and challenge your students to take action if they feel strongly about a cause. At a high school in a small New Mexican town, a journalism teacher grew tired of hearing his students complain that the media only portrayed teens as dropouts, drug users, and gang members. "What are you going to do about it?" he finally challenged them. The students discussed the issue, and decided to invite to class the general manager of the local radio station. After hearing what the students had to say, the manager gave them their own 15-minute radio program, called *Positive Teens,* which he then aired every Friday evening.

7. Use television programs in positive ways by combining them with homework assignments. Ask the students to watch a rerun of *The Cosby Show* and discuss how Theo, Vanessa, or some other character handled a peer pressure situation. Have them watch an episode of *Leave It to Beaver* (1950s), *My Three Sons* (1960s), *The Partridge Family* (1970s), *The Cosby Show* (1980s), and *Roseanne* (1990s); follow up the assignment by discussing the family situations on these shows, including the positive and negative parenting techniques, societal pressures, and parental expectations.

8. When discussing with your students the harmful effects of alcohol and other drugs, don't focus only on the results of heavy usage (e.g., cirrhosis of the liver, brain damage, death). Talk about the dangers of light usage, and be sure to explain that these substances have a quicker effect on a brain and body that is still growing.

9. Provide students with healthy role models. Find adults in your community who have worked hard to achieve their goals, and invite them to speak to your class. Draw on resources such as Career Day, monitoring programs, professional speakers, and even visiting parents.

10. Consider using parents, senior citizens, and older students as tutors, reading assistants, or "just friends" for your class. This can be as effective in secondary school as it is in elementary school.

11. Encourage students to develop their powers of observation and critical thinking. Have them study the lyrics of selected rock and rap music; then lead a discussion about the social value of those lyrics. Ask the class to point out the groups that advocate healthy lifestyles and seem to care about their listeners. Make sure students understand the importance of distinguishing those groups from the ones that advocate violence, suicide, drugs, and hatred toward women. This type of exercise can also be used with commercials or magazine advertisements, to teach students how to think critically as consumers. It can help them understand that a certain brand of jeans or deodorant probably isn't going to increase their popularity with true friends.

12. Make your students feel special by once a month baking a birthday cake for all those born that month (don't forget the summer months!). Sing "Happy Birthday"; then get to the classwork.

13. Encourage volunteer work—at senior citizen homes, hospitals, animal shelters, park departments, and so forth. It really helps young people to see there is a lot going on in the world other than what just revolves around them. In fact, a few high schools are now requiring that students complete 12 hours of community service in order to pass health class.

Add some of your own ideas about how you can tone down negative societal effects on your students:

✍

✍

✍

✍

Peer Pressure and the PPR Skill

The three most common characteristics of the child who is most likely to be affected by our societal structure, and most vulnerable to peer pressure, are (1) boredom or apathy, (2) little family time, and (3) low self-image. (Note, however, that any one of these characteristics will often fit most young people.) Children are also highly vulnerable in the first year of a new school. Watch out for the first years of middle school, high school, and college! And remember, it's critical to understand how at-risk your children are!

Every child is better armed to resist peer pressure when he or she is equipped with the PPR skill. Without it, even the best-behaved child, when pressured, is likely to make poor decisions now and then, or to fall short of acting on good decisions. Although such incidents may happen only occasionally, any incident like this is damaging—and unnecessary now that PPR is available to you.

Why is your child likely to make poor decisions occasionally, no matter how well behaved he or she usually is? Because poor behavioral decisions are usually made in *the presence of others,* and your child is exposed to peers daily. It's fascinating to think about the times we've made a poor decision or seen someone else do so. Rarely do people make poor decisions when on their own, without others' influence. Our general survival instincts are pretty good, but it's hard to hear them over the din made by peers trying to talk us out of them! Significantly, most young people are arrested for acts committed when in the company of "friends."

Rarely does trouble occur because a person was physically forced into poor behavior. More commonly, we allow another person to appeal to our emotions, sometimes with good intentions and other times not, but often with poor results. The following remarks are classic examples of the appeals that children hear from their peers. Do any of these "blackmail threats" sound familiar?

— "You're chicken" (the put-down).

— "Grow up" (sarcasm).

— "It'll be fun—we won't get caught"(promise of excitement with no consequences).

25

— "I thought you were my friend" (moral derision and guilt tripping).

— "You won't be popular . . . cool . . . part of the group" (fear of rejection).

To children, remarks like these threaten what they view as their survival. That's when healthy instincts are overruled and the child makes a poor decision and chooses trouble. (Later in this book we will take a close look at the many good PPR responses that children can use to resist this and other forms of manipulation.)

It is important to remember that the resulting trouble is not solely the fault of the child who exerted the peer pressure. Responsibility for the poor decision and its unpleasant consequences rests in part with the decision-maker, the "go-alonger," the child who failed to resist the pressure. If we blame only the leader—the child who instigated the problem—we teach the follower that he or she can get away with improper behavior simply by pointing a finger at someone else.

Of course, good decision making begins with good values, and most parents try to teach their children the difference between right and wrong. Unfortunately, while children can *memorize* what their parents want them to do (or not to do), they *understand the concept of consequences* far better than they understand the concept of morality.

"Knowing" the difference between right and wrong fosters a child's desire to avoid trouble, but it doesn't help that child visualize the consequences of negative actions or provide that child with practice in how to reverse peer pressure in a realistic way—one that will work in real-life social situations. Thus, although it is essential that children be able to recognize potential trouble and learn to distinguish good decisions from bad ones, unless they are also strongly skilled in PPR they will have difficulty *acting* on those good decisions.

Parents often teach their children two basic versions of the PPR skill: (1) to simply say no, and (2) to avoid, or walk away from, peer pressure situations. These forms of resistance can work in some instances if the child has a good measure of self-confidence. But a weak child often won't use them for fear of appearing unfriendly and becoming unpopular. In situations between close friends or involving popular kids, this fear increases, and it becomes difficult to say no in any form. Walking away from the problem can be difficult, too, and is not always possible if a child is at a sleepover or in a friend's car. Again, children fear being teased or, worse, cut out of the group.

We adults even have trouble saying no or walking away from peer pressure situations. But we have developed numerous variations and alternatives—ways of responding to social pressure without offending our peers—and so can draw on them when we need to. Moreover, adult peers tend to back off when confronted by resistance. This isn't the case with children.

Quite often a child's peers continue to exert pressure despite the resistance, especially if the child is using the "plain vanilla" type of responses above rather than the state-of-the-art versions taught in this book. When that happens, which it regularly does, even that strong child needs more training and additional responses to continue to resist.

By junior high school, peer pressure has already become very intense, and it becomes more so each year as young people become more clever at influencing each other. When your children are faced with the difficulty of handling pressure from all sides—from best friends, boyfriends, girlfriends, and older or popular kids they wish to impress, please, or get along with—they are in a much stronger position to deal well with the pressure, to uphold your family values, if they have the PPR skill and if you are using the parenting techniques in this book.

Children often try, and sometimes succeed, in making adults feel that they are wrong on a particular issue and that the child is right. And sometimes we make the mistake of feeling guilty or putting friendship with our children above guidance. You've probably heard at least one of these examples of a child's pressure: "If you really loved me, you would let me do this. Everybody else's parents are letting them." "I don't know why you make me go to bed so early." "How come I have to come in so early?" "You're mean. I hate you." The parental reinforcement outlined in this book will help you handle such manipulation while opening lines of real communication.

We know that resorting to nagging, changing the child's environs instead of the child, or relying on outside authorities to control the child don't work. If they did, we wouldn't have the peer pressure problems growing in this society. Simple techniques such as PPR, bolstered by parental reinforcement, produce results.

Each good decision and every instance of avoided trouble provide the child with achievement feedback and reinforce responsible behavior and strong character. By following the instructions in this book, you and the child will rehearse some trouble situations so that the child can practice making good decisions and taking action to avoid trouble. And you will learn how to reinforce that behavior on an ongoing basis, while fostering the child's good self-image.

In addition to providing you with ways to strengthen your child's sense of responsibility, this book gives you step-by-step techniques—not vague theories!—to reduce and control the pressure in your child's peer group(s), as well as to influence the child's choice of friends and activities. Remember: You *can* regain control of the family.

If you are an educator or other professional helper working with young people, you may want to read the book with a view to teaching young people the PPR skill and to acquainting their parents with the reinforcing parenting techniques.

You may want to overview the book quickly, in its entirety, and then go back and work your way through it, chapter by chapter. There is a lot of material here to digest, and it is inadvisable to swallow it all at once. After you read a chapter, think about it and then test it out. Spend a week or two using the new skill before you go on to another chapter. And take the time to enjoy the results!

2. PEER PRESSURE REVERSAL (PPR):

An Essential Skill to Give a Child

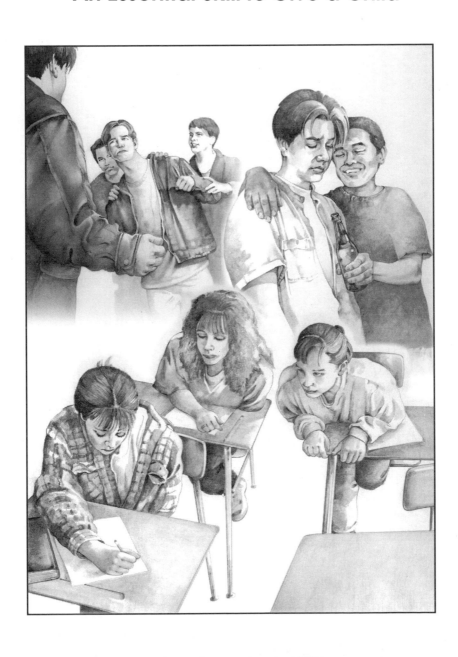

When they're caught in a peer-engineered trap, children can free themselves by making use of the simple, three-step skill called Peer Pressure Reversal (PPR).

This skill is to be taught to the child by an adult—whether a parent, guardian, relative, counselor, teacher, Scout leader, or youth director. Children should not be handed this guidebook and expected to learn on their own; it's not written for a young person's level of vocabulary, understanding, or interest. Should you want a book for children to read on this subject as you teach them, consider using these resources:

- *How to Say No and Keep Your Friends*, Second Edition, for grades 5–12.

- *Too Smart for Trouble*, for grades K–4.

(See the "Resources" section of this guidebook for ordering information.)

First, you, the adult, need to understand and learn the "nuts and bolts" of the three steps of the PPR skill. Then, either in Chapter 3 (for parents) or Chapter 4 (for educators and other professional helpers), you will be shown how to deliver this PPR skill to the child.

If you catch yourself thinking *ahead* of the three PPR steps—to how you will actually teach the steps and make them stick, and what you can do about the child's activities and friends—*stop!* As stated, we'll cover all that at a later point in the book, where you'll learn step-by-step ways to accomplish those goals too. Make it easy on yourself by taking it one chapter—and goal—at a time.

When PPR is taught to the younger child from kindergarten through fourth grade, the skill is simplified in vocabulary and peer pressure examples used. Appropriate comments will be designated by the phrase **Special Note for the Young Child.**

Now, let's start with your mastery of the three-step skill of Peer Pressure Reversal itself.

What are the three PPR steps? They are as follows:

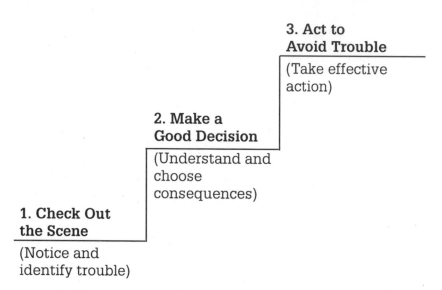

**3. Act to
Avoid Trouble**

(Take effective
action)

**2. Make a
Good Decision**

(Understand and
choose
consequences)

**1. Check Out
the Scene**

(Notice and
identify trouble)

Special Note for the Young Child:

When teaching PPR to a child from kindergarten through fourth grade, Peer Pressure Reversal is called **Too Smart for Trouble**. The three-step skill is the same in content, but the wording is simplified, as shown below:

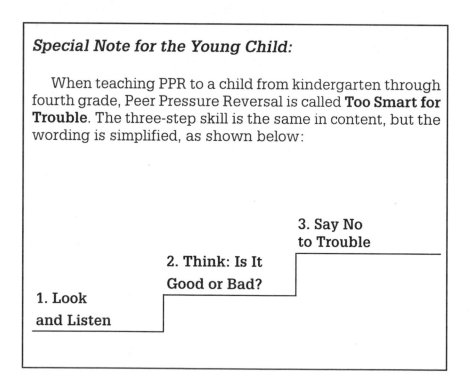

**3. Say No
to Trouble**

**2. Think: Is It
Good or Bad?**

**1. Look
and Listen**

There's nothing too difficult here and plenty of good, common sense. Basically, we want children to **Notice** the trouble situation, which helps them to **Understand** its consequences for them, so that they are able to take appropriate **Action** to protect themselves from unpleasant consequences.

For example, most children get into trouble when peers challenge them with taunts such as "Chicken?" or "Mama's baby!" The typical defense is "No, I'm not," which is usually ineffective, since it's an opening for the friend to influence the child with additional comments like "Prove it!" PPR gives children a selection of effective responses to reverse peer pressure.

You may feel more encouraged to work on the PPR skill with your child if you bear in mind that this skill will improve the quality of life for both your child and your family. How does it accomplish this "miracle"? As the child makes better decisions and becomes more responsible, you begin to trust the child more and to grant more freedom and privileges. As a result, there is less conflict in the family, and everyone is happier.

How does the PPR skill make the child more responsible? It heightens awareness, develops good judgment, and increases self-esteem, self-discipline, and strength of character. It extends the child's ability to take action quickly and direct his or her own moves constructively.

PPR Step 1: Check Out the Scene

When a child finds herself in a peer pressure situation, the first step that she should take is to open up her eyes, ears, and mind to "scope out" the scene. Why? She needs to become a "trouble detective" before she acts.

She must learn to recognize when trouble is imminent, so she can "head the villains off at the pass" before the trouble actually develops. After all, if she doesn't realize she's being manipulated, she isn't going to know enough to take action to avert the trouble. There are many clues a child can learn to read that will alert her to situations that may become trouble for her.

When she starts noticing trouble approaching, or when she realizes that she is caught in the middle of an unexpected trouble situation, she will have to react quickly. It's not only important that she gets in the habit of recognizing potential trouble, but also important that she learns to recognize it early. The faster she is able to pick up on the clues, the more time she will have for planning her strategy and acting upon it. If she's quick enough, she can even avoid a confrontation altogether, giving her peers little opportunity to invite her into trouble to begin with.

To help your child become an alert detective, make sure that she knows, and feels comfortable with, the two substeps of PPR Step 1:

Check Out the Scene

- **Look and Listen**

  (Better awareness of others and the environment)
- **Apply the "Trouble?" Rule**

  (Recognition of potential trouble to be avoided)

By mastering and getting into the habit of using these two "Check Out" substeps, your child will be more aware of her environment, and have more time to make good decisions and to act upon them, thereby avoiding trouble whenever possible.

Special Note for the Young Child:

PPR Step 1 is called **Look and Listen**.

The following substeps would be simplified for the grade K–4 child. It will help the child to understand what trouble clues to look and listen for if you demonstrate each one. The young ones often "stumble" into trouble because they are not paying attention and miss important cues.

Look and Listen

Observe Friends Objectively

A child needs to **look** at the **appearance and behavior** of his friends (or other peers) in the situation of the moment. Is there anything unusual or suspicious in the way they are grouped, postured, dressed, or acting, or in the things they are doing? Are they huddled in a group looking to see if anyone is watching? Is one child giggling nervously as he talks? Is another whispering secretively?

Look Around at the Surroundings

He should also **look** at the appearance of the **environment** around the group. Are they in a place or a set-up that tempts trouble—such as an unoccupied house or apartment, a deserted street or school, a club where no one's checking ID's, a dark building, an area of land with a No Trespassing sign, or a party without chaperons or with mostly older kids— or in a situation where he can see trouble actually happening as he watches?

Listen Between the Lines

The child should **listen** to what his peers are talking about, and be on the alert for their hints and suggestions. He should try to understand what is being implied—what is meant but not actually put into words. Peers may try to talk him into trouble by using a "sales pitch," or they may try to pressure him if they find that easier than being persuasive. They may avoid directly answering any questions that ask for more details.

If the peer is a friend and the child knows him well, is that friend speaking in an unusual way? It is sometimes easier for a child to detect peer pressure when he is with close friends, although whether or not the child knows his peers well, he can still listen for words or lines that sound like a sales pitch or exert pressure. He can ask himself, "Are they trying to persuade me with bribing . . . lure me with fantasies . . . blackmail me with friendship . . . pressure me with scorn?" When people try to sell someone on an idea or pressure him to adopt their way of thinking, they don't speak in their normal, matter-of-fact way. They give their "victim" special attention, and they tend to speak more dramatically than usual.

First Impressions

When friends look, speak, or act suspiciously, a child should avoid rationalizing away doubts and suspicions. These are the first clues that indicate trouble. Instead, the child should make an extra effort to be conscious of the way her friends are acting and of how a scene looks and sounds. She should go with her first, gut-level reaction. It's usually the right reaction, since it takes place before she has had time to make excuses for the people she likes. Yes, it's difficult to look and listen objectively, but it provides helpful clues to potential trouble.

The Sell

The child is probably familiar with at least one, if not all, of these opening lines from typical peer-pressure sales pitches: "Hey, I've got an idea!" "Do you wanna . . . ?" "Let's (do such and such)." Although the same lines can be used to suggest positive activities too, it is no less crucial for your child to consider them clues to potential trouble. She should go on the alert when she hears them and stay alert for what follows the pitch. What is important here is that your children learn how to listen for **invitations** to trouble.

The Pressure

The child has probably also heard all of these opening lines of peer pressure: "*Everybody's* doing it." "We won't get caught." "It's no big deal." "Hey, be cool." "You chicken?" "Scared?" "If you're really my friend, you'll do this with me." "Mama's baby." "I'll give you some money if you'll do this for me." "Aw, you're a real wimp, aren't you?" "Grow up!" "I won't invite you to my birthday party if you don't do this with me." "If you really loved me, you would do this." And so on. It's more obvious to the child that *these* lead-ins are likely to spell trouble. People don't use these lines to get us to do things that are acceptable.

Look and Listen Demonstration #1

An older child is invited to a friend's house for a party—an informal gathering. He is following the **Look and Listen** substep of **Check Out the Scene**.

As he walks in, he notices his surroundings. Are the rooms dimly lit? How many people are present? Are there any adults present? Does he know the kids, and are they okay kids? Does he recognize any known troublemakers?

He also notices the appearance and behavior of the people in the room. Do the kids seem concerned about who's walking in the door (as if they're scared it may be an adult)? Do they look as though they're talking and interacting in a normal way, or does he see appearances or actions that clue him in to trouble?

The presence of alcohol is commonly indicated by the way guests look and act: they may have bloodshot eyes, alcohol on their breath, be overly loud, and even stagger or fall as they try to move around. If guests are sharing marijuana, they may be somewhat lethargic—just sitting around and listening to music. The room may be smoky; perhaps cigarettes are being openly passed. When a cigarette is passed around a room, the chances are strong that it's a marijuana joint.

When he walks into the party, he also pays attention to what's being offered to him and the other guests for fun. Is he being invited to drink alcohol or use other drugs, for example?

Look and Listen Demonstration #2

A child is walking home from visiting friends. As she's walking down the street, she sees, a block ahead, some kids who are certain trouble. They're huddled together under a streetlight that appears to have been knocked out.

She is too far away from the group to learn anything by listening, but by looking over the set-up and being observant, she can see that there may be trouble and that she needs to take another route to avoid it.

Apply the "Trouble?" Rule

Once the child has done the **Look and Listen** substep of **Check Out the Scene**, he is ready to move on to the **"Trouble?" Rule**. Having fully observed what is happening in a situation, he must ask these two questions:

- Does it break a law?
- Will it make an authority angry?

Asking and answering the **"Trouble?" Rule** questions helps your child decide whether the situation will actually result in trouble. Guesswork and uncertainty are minimized, and your child can feel more self-confident about his ability to make such decisions.

We must remember, however, that as important as these questions are, they only take a child so far. They simply help him identify *when* he is in a situation that requires him to be on the alert; they do not help him identify or understand what the consequences of the trouble will be.

"Trouble?" Rule Question #1

"Does It Break a Law?"

Whether or not a child believes a law to be right and fair, breaking it can bring her unpleasant consequences. She could get arrested, have to pay a fine, suffer social humiliation, have to spend time in a correctional facility, acquire a police record that can affect her for life, and so forth. So asking this question can remind and warn a child that she's facing serious trouble when the answer is "yes."

What are some actions by young people that constitute breaking the law? Stealing, failure to attend school, drinking alcohol when under the legal age, driving while intoxicated, possession or use of illegal drugs, assault, burglary, arson, carrying concealed weapons, driving without a license, prank calls, and vandalism are some examples.

"Trouble?" Rule Question #2

"Will It Make an Authority Angry?"

Again, whether or not the child agrees with the authority in control, if he does something that angers that authority, he is likely to get caught eventually and suffer unpleasant consequences. These consequences can include loss of adult trust and respect, his privileges, and his self-esteem, all of which he enjoys. When he loses the trust of adults, he hears more "no" responses to his requests than "yes."

Who are the people in control? When we talk here about someone in control, we do not include dominant peers or older playmates. Rather, we mean parents, teachers, principals, shopowners, coaches, relatives, babysitters, homeowners, police, employers, youth leaders, friends' parents, and so forth. The child with a religious upbringing may also consider a "Supreme Being" an authority who can be upset. No matter what our age, we all have authority figures in our lives, as we all have rules we must follow to maintain a safe and rational society.

Sometimes children give in to group peer pressure. This form of peer pressure, which emphasizes conformity to the group, is often more implied than openly verbalized (unless, of course, a child in the group resists it). Such pressure commonly includes fear of change, fear of standing out from the crowd, fear of being associated with someone who is not popular and of being "contaminated" with that unpopularity, and other such pressures.

Giving in to this pressure results in selfish and unkind behavior. "Do unto others as you would have them do unto you" is a universal law of human decency. When children have trouble observing this "law," authorities get upset. There are negative consequences, such as loss of privileges and self-esteem, for the child who acts under the influence of such pressure.

Here are some examples of how a child can be controlled by group peer pressure.

- She sees an unpopular classmate crying in the school bathroom, and she doesn't offer help or, at the least, a gesture of sympathy.

- He sees a child often eating alone in the cafeteria or sitting alone on the school bus, and he doesn't try to help that child be included.

- He sees drugs being sold to a child and is scared to report it.

- She ignores, gets her clique to ignore, and perhaps even spreads gossip or rumors about someone new who looks snobby or nerdy. Or she does the same to someone she knows because she is mad at her.

- He sees someone trying to start a fight with, or picking on, someone "weaker," and he doesn't get help, or intervene as a group, or try to distract the bully. Perhaps he even stands around and watches or encourages others who are ganging up on the child.

- She tears down a rival to make herself look good.

However, group peer pressure of this kind doesn't only promote unkindness to peers who stand outside the group. Oftentimes it also acts as a catalyst that prompts children to cause trouble in ways they may not have thought of on their own, or that provokes them to act on an idea they wouldn't have carried out on their own even if they had thought of it. Such behavior would include breaking a law or, essentially, doing anything that angers authority.

The consequences for the child can make him feel uncomfortable with himself, humiliated, guilty, or sad. Being on the receiving end of disappointment from parents, teachers, employers, relatives, and the law doesn't build self-esteem and happiness any more than does losing privileges.

So if a child's answer to the second question of the **"Trouble?" Rule**—Will it make an authority angry?—is "yes," then the child is warned that there may be trouble for him if he gets involved in the activity.

Apply the "Trouble?" Rule Demonstration

It doesn't take much imagination to think of many ways a young person might anger authorities, break a law, and damage self-esteem. Some typical examples follow:

- Talking during class while the teacher is teaching or while the students are studying or taking tests. This is unacceptable to the teacher.

- Skipping "just one" class at school. This gets a number of people in control angry: teacher, principal, parent, and school counselor. It also breaks a law.

- Staying out an hour past the stated curfew. This gets someone in control—the parent—angry.

- Being dropped off at a theater to watch an approved movie, but going instead to see an unapproved one, or waiting a few minutes and then exiting to go somewhere off-limits. This is unacceptable to the theater staff and the parents.

See the following lists for additional examples of behavior that earn a "yes" answer to either or both of the two **"Trouble?" Rule** questions.

For the Younger Child

Riding a friend's bicycle without asking permission

Riding a bicycle in an off-limits area

Snooping in an open garage

Making prank phone calls

Stealing candy or toys

Running in the halls at school

Cutting into the school cafeteria line

Taking change left on lunch table

Playing with matches

Name-calling

Fighting

Shooting off fireworks

Playing with a parent's gun

Swimming without adult supervision

Smoking cigarettes

Lying to parents about homework

Going too far from home

Teasing someone in unkind ways

Cheating on school work

Damaging neighbors' holiday decorations

For the Older Child

Cheating during a test

Lying to parents about plans with peers

Copying homework

Drinking alcohol

Smoking marijuana

Smoking cigarettes/ Using smokeless tobacco

Doing pills

Stealing cigarettes/cosmetics/jewelry/clothes

Breaking into a vending machine

Stealing parent's money

Taking parent's car without permission

Sneaking out at night

Forging parent's signature on note or report card

Driving a car without a license

Driving with beginner's license but unaccompanied by licensed driver

Riding with an unlicensed driver

Drag racing

Having a party when parents are gone

Loaning money

Skipping school

Leaving school grounds at lunch

Buying alcohol underage

Going to a bar underage

Experimenting with sex

Hiding a runaway

Entering a vacant apartment or building

Harassing a teacher

Carrying a weapon

Stealing supplies from employer

Damaging others' property

"Wrapping" someone's house

"Spiking" punch at a dance

Getting in a car with unfamiliar kids

Skipping sports practice

Bragging about dating exploits

Instigating a fight

Joining a gang

Cussing

Passing a note during class

Cutting someone out of the "group"

Double-dating with someone you don't like

PPR Step 2: Make a Good Decision

The second PPR step for the child—after he has checked out the scene—is to make a good decision if he has detected signs of trouble. This involves identifying and understanding the potential consequences of the situation and committing to his decisions about it. This must be done before he can take action to reverse peer pressure.

Before the child learned how to use PPR Step 1, **Check Out the Scene**, he might have been led unknowingly into trouble. Now that Step 1 has made him aware of trouble situations, he can choose to avoid trouble. He can make this conscious choice by going through the two thought processes in PPR Step 2, **Make a Good Decision**, rather than being manipulated. He can make a responsible decision in time to act on it.

In PPR Step 2, the child first identifies the pros and cons of the consequences—what is likely to happen if he follows his peer's suggestion. After he has weighed both sides of the consequences, he then chooses between them, basing his decision on *logic* and *what's right,* not emotion.

Through these two thought processes, he is able to view his options and to figure out which choice is the best one for him. It's not enough for a child to be skilled in recognizing a trouble situation; he must know how to think in terms of *consequences* if he is to decide on, and follow through on, the safest course of action to take.

Make a Good Decision

- **Weigh Both Sides**

  (Identify and understand the pros and cons of the trouble's consequences)

- **Decide: Stop or Go**

  (Make and commit to a choice)

Special Note for the Young Child:

PPR Step 2 is called **Think: Is It Good or Bad**?

What is difficult for the young ones to understand is that their friends do not *make* them do wrong things. Their friends may ask, suggest, encourage, or beg, but that's not making them do it. They need to clearly understand that they have a choice.

Weigh Both Sides

Before the child makes her choice of whether or not to do what her friends want her to do, she needs to weigh both sides. She needs to identify and understand the consequences and the weight—both the positive and the negative—of the action she is considering, so that her decision will be an informed and intelligent one. She needs to ask herself, "If I do it, what good could happen? If I do it, what bad could happen?"

The Up Side

When a child's friends are trying to talk her into trouble, which side are the friends going to build up? The good side, of course: all the reasons why she will enjoy going and doing the "it" with them. They can be very appealing and often sound like fun. They may include a subtle threat of the loss of something pleasant (popularity, status, or acceptance). Friends often say things such as "Everyone's doing it," or "If you were my friend, then you would do this with me." The child may go along to please her friend to try to keep a friendship intact.

The Down Side

To balance the benefits of going along with the friend's suggestion, the child needs to mentally list all the unpleasant consequences that could happen. He can't rely solely on what his friends tell him about the "up" side when making a decision. Granted, the negative consequences might not happen; but there is a chance they will.

The negative consequences generally fall into these categories: disappointing parents; losing parents' and other authorities' trust, and having pleasures and privileges taken away; developing a bad reputation; losing good friends and acquiring poor ones; causing troubled relations with adults; undergoing suspension or expulsion from school; suffering social humiliation; getting physically hurt; being arrested; being penalized with fines or extra work; damaging self-respect.

The Sum Total

As the child mentally examines the lists of pleasures the trouble would bring versus the possible pains, the pain list is always longer or carries more weight. The child needs to think logically and quickly, rather than think emotionally as the pressuring peer wants! In other words, the child needs to listen to herself and to trust that "voice" inside.

Weigh Both Sides Demonstration #1

A child is asked by a peer to skip sixth-period class with him. His friend tells him, "It's only art. We're not going to do anything in class today anyway, so why not? We'll go to my house and have a soft drink."

The child recognizes potential trouble (PPR Step 1) and then considers the pros and cons (PPR Step 2).

He identifies the good things that could happen: he wouldn't have to go to art class, he would get to have a soft drink with his friend, and he would have some fun with his friend.

He then identifies the bad things that could happen if he skips sixth period with his friend: as he leaves school he could get caught by the principal, who would give him detention and/or call his parents, who would also punish him. He might get caught by the friend's mom, who would call his parents. The art teacher might give a class assignment, and he would miss it. He might get picked up by the truant officer as he leaves school. He might start to develop a reputation as a kid who will skip school, and other children who skip school may coerce or tease him to join them in that activity.

He realizes that the con list is much longer than the pro list.

Weigh Both Sides Demonstration #2

A child has arrived early at school, and a peer invites her to go behind the school building to smoke a cigarette.

She notices potential trouble (PPR Step 1) and weighs both the pros and cons (PPR Step 2). The good that could happen would be that she would have a moment of feeling "cool" by smoking and being free from adult restrictions, as well as having fun with her friend.

The bad that could happen might include getting disciplined at school. Also, her parents might be called, feel disappointed in her, and discipline her at home. She will smell bad. She will be harming her own health and her appearance with cigarettes.

Suddenly her friend doesn't seem very smart after all.

Decide: Stop or Go

Now that the child has developed a complete mental picture of the consequences versus benefits, he needs to decide which way he wants to act: avoid trouble or risk it. He has to choose.

He has to think first, "Is it worth it?"— and secondly, "Now choose."

Many times children will think of the consequences but then decide that they won't get caught or that they're willing to take the risk. They need to consider that there's always a chance they will get caught, and to imagine what those consequences would really feel like should they choose to go along with their friends. They may at first be willing to risk the consequences, but if they visualize themselves suffering the consequences, they often decide they're not willing after all. Most children also realize they will suffer unpleasant guilt feelings when they make a poor decision but don't get caught.

When the child has completely weighed the heavy consequences against the lighter pleasures, he will usually choose to forego the trouble for the best of reasons: to please himself. He's more pleased with avoiding the negative consequences he now recognizes and fears—including his parents removing long-term privileges—than he is with pursuing the lesser, short-term gain offered by his peer. In other words, it isn't worth it, and he chooses to find a way to avoid the trouble. He feels good for doing what's right.

When children consider *all* the risks, they rarely conclude "I want to risk trouble."

This choice to make the responsible decision to avoid trouble is based on their belief that adult authority will administer discipline for unacceptable behavior. Firm yet fair adults help to keep the "consequences scale" balanced for children so that they are motivated to make good decisions.

Decide: Stop or Go Demonstration #1

A friend approaches a child and tries to borrow her homework because he wants to copy it.

The child hears potential trouble (PPR Step 1) and identifies the pros and cons (PPR Step 2) of letting him borrow her paper. The good consequences would likely be that she would feel kind, she would be more popular with him, and he might return the favor.

The bad consequences that she would be risking, and have to be willing to face, if she loaned the homework would include the following: the possibility that he would lose her paper, getting a zero on her homework if they got caught, having to do the work over, being embarrassed if caught, receiving other punishment from the teacher or principal, developing the reputation of someone who cheats, and losing privileges at home if parents are notified. In the long run, she's not even being kind to the borrower, because he won't know the material later when tested on it and very likely would continue to borrow her homework in the future, rather than study and learn.

She chooses which path she will follow in this moment of decision making. She decides she wants to avoid, rather than face, the negative consequences she'd be risking if she gave in to her friend.

Decide: Stop or Go Demonstration #2

A girl is at school during recess with a group of her friends. They're talking about a new girl in school, whom some of the girls do not like because they think she is "stuck-up" and a "goody-goody." This child has to make a decision about whether she will go along with her friends and put this girl down and not talk to her, or whether she is going to give the girl a chance since she really doesn't know her yet, and continue speaking to her.

If she chooses to give the girl a chance, she has just made this decision in her mind: "I'm going to avoid trouble. I'm not going to get involved in a negative situation by being cruel and by talking about other people behind their backs."

PPR STEP 3: ACT TO AVOID TROUBLE

Act to Avoid Trouble is the most important of the three PPR steps that the child takes to reverse peer pressure. The first two PPR steps (both internal thought processes) have prepared the child for this third step. She already looks, listens, applies the **"Trouble?" Rule**, weighs both sides, and decides not to go any further toward the potential trouble. Now she needs to learn how to avoid trouble: how to take constructive *action* in order to resist pressuring peers and to get out of, or stay away from, trouble-threatening situations. Her aim now is to avoid being manipulated.

Young people need a repertoire of responses they can direct at peers in order to reverse peer pressure situations skillfully. It can be done without their losing friends or prestige among peers. It can actually build additional respect, and even admiration, in friends and other peers.

Many young people "go along" with peers in order to be liked and to fit in. Most youngsters abhor standing out from the crowd—being different. Other children go along because they don't want to feel or seem like "nerds."

Young people often pressure themselves to do things they wouldn't do on their own, especially when they get the impression from peers that "everybody's doing it." "Everybody" may just be their own small clique of friends, but the pressure is just as intense. They fear losing their popularity with friends by saying, "No, that's wrong. I'm not going to do that."

If a child isn't overly concerned with what the crowd is doing, he may be challenged by peers who *are* concerned ("Are you chicken?"), or he may fall victim to an alluring sales pitch ("How'd you like to . . . ? It will be fun"). Or the peer may try to control the child and not allow him any freedom to make decisions ("We're going to do this, we're going to do that").

Another commonly used peer pressure technique is to appeal to the responsible side of the child by questioning his loyalty and raising guilt feelings ("If you were really my friend, you'd . . . "). If the peer gets upset because the child won't go along with an idea, what should that tell the child about the peer? The peer is looking for trouble; the peer is afraid to follow through on the idea by himself, because it is wrong and could have negative consequences; the peer wants the child to share that risk; the peer is not being a good friend to the child. The child must be helped to understand this, so that he need not feel guilty about refusing to allow himself to be victimized.

We've now seen that there are many forms of peer pressure. To handle any of them, young people desperately need a variety of quick, clever, and effective responses that they can "whip out" on a moment's notice. Telling young people to just say no is not enough. As the late humorist, Erma Bombeck, wrote in a classic 1989 column, "We are in the throes of a new approach to peer pressure—'Just Say No!' Putting those three little words up against peer pressure is like Pee-Wee Herman facing off with Ted Koppel. How can kids say no when parents can barely say it?"

PPR Step 3, **Act to Avoid Trouble**, answers this need, offering 10 highly practical responses to peer pressure, at least one or more of which should work in any given situation.

Ensure that your child has mastered the first two PPR steps, **Check Out the Scene** and **Make a Good Decision**; then turn to this step for the basic defense tactics that your child can use to "win the battle" against peer pressure— and, indeed, it sometimes seems like an actual battle out there! When adults are introduced to these responses, many express the wish that they had known of them as a child. Some have added that they plan to adopt these responses for their own use when needed with pushy adult friends!

Teach your child these two substeps of PPR Step 3:

Act to Avoid Trouble

- **What to Say**

   (10 response choices)
- **How to Say It**

   (Delivery of responses)

Special Note for the Young Child:

PPR Step 3 is called **Say No to Trouble**. Only 5 of the 10 response choices are taught so as not to overwhelm the child.

What to Say

Following are the 10 PPR response choices. A child very often will use more than one of the responses to get out of a trouble situation with an insistent peer. The aim of the responses is to get the friend away from the trouble, or to get away from the friend! When a child fails to avoid a trouble situation, one or more of these PPR responses can rescue her.

The 10 PPR Responses

1. Simply Say No
2. Leave the Scene
3. Ignore the Peer(s)
4. Make an Excuse
5. Change the Subject
6. Make a Joke
7. Act Shocked
8. Use Flattery
9. Suggest a Better Idea
10. Return the Challenge

Now let's look at these 10 responses individually.

Special Note for the Young Child:

Ten responses are too many to teach the young ones. Teach only half of them (Simply Say No, Leave the Scene, Make a Joke, Suggest a Better Idea, Return the Challenge), plus Tell an Adult, which should be used when the child wants support and always in a dangerous situation (e.g., someone wants the child to play with a gun, to swim without adult supervision, or to play with matches).

---

1. Simply Say No

"Read My Lips!"

Using this basic PPR response, the child simply says no. It's an upfront, honest, and expressly courageous choice. It's simple and effective. It doesn't leave her open to persuasion. It can be done politely. Perhaps surprisingly, it's not used often enough, largely due to lack of self-confidence.

There are many words that convey the message "no" either subtly or straightforwardly; and there are many tones of voice in which to say them. A child's voice and facial expression when delivering that "no" can tell peers how she feels about their pressure as much as her words can. We'll talk more about how to look and speak when using any PPR response. For this "Simply Say No" response, the key is that she keeps it short, sweet, and closed to discussion. She goes right on to something else, making it inarguably clear that *that* particular subject is closed.

When she wants to be her least aggressive and her most tactful, polite, and pleasant, she uses a gentle but firm tone and mannerly words. She ends her "no" statement with the use of the friend's name or nickname, and perhaps softens her "no" in humorous or dramatically exaggerated terms, so the "no" is not heavy and offensive.

When she's being pressured, rather than persuaded, and is less concerned about the others' sensitivity since they're not exhibiting much toward her, she speaks more sternly and briefly, perhaps even sarcastically. She is being firm, and she is letting more of her displeasure show, in proportion to the more serious pressure.

Here are possible "Simply Say No" responses. The tone in which they are said is up to the child. There may be additional responses that she wants to add to her list.

Shake head no.

"No thank you."

"No thanks!"

"Don't think I will."

"Don't get your hopes up."

"Uh-uh."

"Don't want to."

"I don't think so."

"Not today."

"Sorry, Charlie."

"Have a good time."

"That's not one of your all-time great ideas!"

"Not if I want to see tomorrow."

"Forget it, Fred."

"What don't you understand about the word 'no'?"

"Thanks anyway, (name)."

"Don't feel like it."

"I'll pass."

"I'm not really interested."

"Can't."

"I'd rather not."

"That's wrong."

"Next year."

"Forget it."

"Certainly not."

"No way."

"Not if I want to live."

"Nope"

"No."

"No way, José!"

"Not me!"

"Never in a million years."

"That's a dumb idea."

"I'm out."

Children also enjoy learning how to say the word "no" in several foreign languages, such as *nyet* in Russian, *non* in French, *nein* in German, and *ne* in Czech.

"*No way!*"

2. Leave the Scene

"Make Like a Tree, and Leave"

The child may decide that actions speak louder than words and walk away from the trouble situation, even if she's in the middle of it.

She may choose this response for one or more reasons: the peer's suggestion may be so ridiculous, difficult to handle, or upsetting that she feels she either cannot give, or does not want to give, the suggestion her time, attention, and effort. She doesn't even explain her action.

Or she may use this PPR response as a follow-up to one or two other PPR responses if a peer is particularly insistent. In this way, she demonstrates her strength of conviction while also avoiding a serious argument.

> **The Leave the Scene Rule is . . .**
>
> Say "no," using any PPR response, no more than **twice** before you end the discussion and walk away.

She can act offended and walk away. That leaves the peer defensive rather than aggressive. Or she can act bored or preoccupied with something else. Either way, she walks away with her back straight, her head high, exuding obvious pride in herself. Even if she's scared or her feelings are hurt, she should try to act proud of herself. If she's a gentle sort, she may find it easier to project that "stiff upper lip" if she can express a little self-righteous anger or disgust in self-defense.

She may choose to leave more casually, perhaps with a little shake of the head, as if she can't believe that the peer even suggested such a silly idea. Then she can casually saunter off. It's important that she exit proudly, so she doesn't give the impression of vulnerability. Otherwise, the peer may go after her or try to pressure her at another time.

It's important that she does leave the area completely and not return immediately. It's critical that the child not "yo-yo" when leaving the scene. To "yo-yo" is when the child has walked away from the trouble invitation, but turns and walks back toward the pressuring peer who is verbalizing reasons why the child should go along. Later, in role-playing practices between you and the child, the child should actually turn and walk away. This is difficult body language for many children, and practice helps strengthen their use of it.

3. Ignore the Peer(s)

"Ignorance Can Be Bliss"

The child can ignore the peer's pressuring comment or suggestion. He can appear involved in something—his studies, his thoughts, someone else's conversation, what the teacher is saying, the music he is listening to, or the show that he is watching—and totally disregard the source of trouble.

This response can be used when a peer in the classroom is trying to instigate a child to talk, pass notes, show test answers, and so forth. If the child even makes eye contact or whispers to the peer, "Ssh, we're not supposed to be talking," he will lose the advantages of the "Ignore" response. Also, the teacher might catch them talking at just that moment. Ignoring the peer is the best, and perhaps the only risk-free, response to such a classroom situation.

This is also an effective tactic when a peer is making negative comments about the child to the world at large, or when peers are exchanging such comments in a group, and the child doesn't want to be drawn into the weak position of defending or explaining himself.

The child should walk or sit tall and proud, with head held high. It's best if he busies himself in a conversation with someone else, or in an activity. If the problem occurs on a school bus, he should focus on packing up his things and be ready to get off the bus quickly when it stops. (The next day the child could try to sit toward the front of the bus, closer to the driver, to avoid a repeat problem.)

If he continues to be pressured, there are many other PPR responses he could use to deal with the problem.

4. Make an Excuse

"Excuses, Excuses"

This is children's Number One choice of response to peer pressure, often for want of diverse ideas. You may think that your advice on how to use this response is unnecessary because your children are so familiar with using it. Actually, you can help them keep their excuses as honest as possible, and show them that it is an adult skill they can master.

The excuse is an adult skill in the sense that adults use it regularly and constructively to ease difficult situations in which someone's feelings can be hurt. Ordinarily, no one is hurt by an excuse, and often feelings are spared. Think of how you might use an excuse. Perhaps you don't care to accept a dinner invitation, for instance, and rather than being brutally blunt and honest, explaining that you don't care to spend time with the host, you make the excuse that you have other commitments that evening or are generally busy during this period of time.

Excuses should be based on truth. The child needs to be told that the more truthful the excuse, the better it works. One reason it works better is that the child states it more convincingly than a fib, so the peer accepts it more readily. Another is that the child's sense of self-esteem isn't threatened, as with "fibbing." And a third reason is that it doesn't come back to haunt the child later when an excuse has a basis in fact.

In many situations, a child may feel he can't use a simple "no." He may have an advanced case of hero worship or "puppy love" for a peer. Or he may be afraid of hurting sensitive feelings, especially those of people he's close to. Or he may simply find that the basic "no thanks" doesn't suit his personality. Even though he may feel okay about refusing a good friend's effort to pressure him into a trouble situation, he may want to choose a PPR response less assertive than "no" to avoid the trouble.

Whatever the case, the important issue is that your child is trying to be strong enough to stay out of peer-induced trouble.

Here are some examples of effective excuses:

"I just got off being grounded and can't take the risk."

"I've got homework."

"I haven't got time."

"My mother (father) would kill me."

"I'd like to be able to say yes, but I just can't."

"I've got to babysit."

"I've got my orthodontist appointment today."

"I've already made plans."

"I've promised my little brother (little sister) that . . ."

"I'm expecting a phone call."

"I've got to go to_____" (soccer practice, piano lessons, work, etc.).

"I don't have any money and don't want to borrow some because I'm already in hock" (or, "There's something I'm saving for").

"My parents are waiting for me."

"I'm supposed to be meeting somebody shortly."

"I'm tired."

"I don't feel well."

"I don't feel like it."

"I'm not in the mood."

"I've got a million chores to do and will get in trouble if they're not done. Gotta go."

And then there's the sure-fire excuse: "I've got to go to the bathroom. See you later." He can take his time there in order to lose the peer. Few people follow you into the bathroom to try to talk you into trouble!

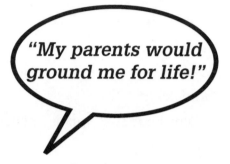

"*My parents would ground me for life!*"

5. Change the Subject

"The Switch"

When a peer suggests trouble, the child may choose to change the subject. The Switch must be surprising, startling, dramatic. It can be shockingly personal, gruesome, scary, or unexpected. It works best if it's *about the peer,* rather than about others. (The child doesn't want to appear a gossip.)

"Guess what Bill said about you! It's all over school." The peer will usually be distracted enough to ask, "What?" The child answers something like, "He said you have really beautiful eyes."

Here's another example: "Guess what I just heard about you! It's all over school." (Waits for "What?" response.) "A guy said that you have the best pitching arm in the school."

A child could also start off with "Did you see that gross story on the news?" ("on TV," "in the paper," etc.).

The technique is to say something out of the ordinary to totally change the subject and to cause the peer to be taken aback; then to keep him on the new track so he doesn't return to the peer pressure situation. Or the child can begin talking about a favorite subject of the peer (e.g., cars, clothes, sports) as a distraction. This technique is a natural for children who have "motor mouths."

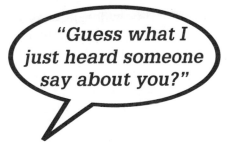

"Guess what I just heard someone say about you?"

6. Make a Joke

"Humor Is Good Medicine"

Saying "no" in joking ways can lighten the pressure and the atmosphere of a peer situation. It can take the sting out of a child's refusal to go along with a friend, while still making it clear that the peer's suggestion was not worth seriously discussing. The child can even choose to keep the joke rolling with dramatic elaboration or more silly lines, just to be sure he's past the danger point. He can simultaneously keep his peer's friendship by being "cool" and witty.

A joke can distract, disarm, and even deflate a friend who's trying to persuade a child to make a poor decision. Few people, young or old, can resist appreciating a good joke or booing a corny one. Teasing or jokes often act as a diversion from the topic of trouble, and can even make a peer more receptive to the child's way of thinking. Even when the peer is aware of what the child is doing, the peer often doesn't resent it, because it's fun being entertained.

Children like to give (and receive) this kind of response, because they feel secure that they will not be seen as harsh, stubborn, judgmental, or negative by a joking turn-aside or turn-down.

If quick wit or a good sense of humor is genuinely not the child's style, he can develop a few standard jokes or teasing expressions that are genuinely funny and that he can remember for future use.

If he tries them out and falls flat, he may want to work on his delivery at times when not so much is on the line, until it is good enough to carry him through a difficult situation.

Whether your child already has a well-developed sense of humor or not, remember: he doesn't have to be a monologue master like Jay Leno or a one-liner whiz like David Letterman to use this response. He can be a bit goofy and still inject a little humor into the situation. And if he has a strong sense of humor, he'll really take to this way of deflecting peer pressure.

Here are some examples of trouble suggestions and playful responses:

Asked to go somewhere he shouldn't . . .

"I'd love to, but I've got plans. I've got to rearrange my sock drawer."

"I'd love to, but I need to spend more time with my plants."

"Love to, but it's my night to brush my dog's teeth!"

"Rats, that's the same night as my Hollywood screen test."

Asked to share a joint (or other drugs) . . .

"Is that a low-tar joint? I only smoke low-tar joints."

"I'm waiting for the latest Surgeon General's report."

"I just popped a few M&M's; I can't handle any more today."

Asked to take a drink of alcohol . . .

"Not my brand."

"That idea is one taco short of a combination plate!"

"I'm allergic. Gives me prickly heat." (or, "Turns my skin green.")

"Sure, if you think you'll like watching me barf in your car."

"I never drink before I'm drunk."

Asked to do something he shouldn't . . .

"No dahling, I prefer to remain a mystery."

"Can't. NASA's expecting me to take a look at some moon rocks."

"If I did that, my reputation might improve."

"I never go out on days that end in 'y'."

"I'd love to, but I promised my gerbil I'd rollerblade with him tonight."

7. Act Shocked

"I Can't Believe It!"

The child is amazed, amused, astounded. Or at least she acts like she is! Her eyes roll up or bug out, and her mouth drops open. She may not look her most attractive, but she makes her point. A little friendly, joking sarcasm is the secret ingredient. Then she adds a phrase like:

> "Oh, sure. Just what I always wanted to do."

> "I can't believe what I just heard."

> "I can't even believe you suggested that."

> "I know you didn't mean that."

> "You didn't really say that, did you? There's a ventriloquist in the house."

> "What a nutty idea."

> "Why did I pick such a goofy friend? Just lucky, I guess?"

> "How childish."

> "How silly."

> "Earth calling_____."

> "That idea's a little too scatterbrained even for me."

> "Where do you get your ideas? You must watch the Looney Tunes on Saturday morning."

Whatever she says, she leaves the friend enough room to back off and to save face by saying something such as, "I was just joking," or "Yeah, I guess that would be kind of dumb."

"I can't believe you suggested that!"

8. Use Flattery

"Flattery Can Get You Somewhere"

What a pleasant way to get out of a tight spot. The child doesn't want to antagonize his friend or admired acquaintance, or perhaps he doesn't want to stir up the ire of a particularly fearsome bully. Instead of ignoring or confronting the trouble suggestion, he may want to flatter his way out of it. He feels warm for saying kind things, and he's equally happy to have escaped from between a rock and a hard place!

It's so simple and yet works so beautifully. People don't get enough compliments in this world, and almost everyone is susceptible to praise that falls their way. All the way back to the ancient fable of the fox and the crow, clever people have used flattery to control troublesome associates.

If the child is concerned that using flattery is sneaky, she can remind herself that (1) the strokes are pleasant for the peer, and (2) she's helped both herself and the peer avoid trouble. This is a very constructive and easy response. With a minimum of practice, it can become automatic and roll easily off the tongue.

If the child really can't think of something about the peer to praise, particularly on short notice, then she may want to use a tried-and-true flattery line that she has cultivated. Here are some examples. The child can take them and "run" with them, tailoring her flattery to the individual situation.

> "You're too smart to really mean that."

> "You usually have much better ideas."

> "You're too important to me for me to let you do that."

> "You're too good a friend; I don't want to see you hurt" ("get in trouble," "lose privileges," etc.).

> "I know you can come up with something better than that idea!"

> "Hey, I really like you. I want us to be able to stay friends."

> "You know better!"

"If we got caught, my parents wouldn't let me do things with you anymore. I'd hate that."

"You have such a great brain. Can't you think of something more fun than that?" (Or, "Can't you think of something nice to say about her?")

If the peer can't be talked out of her idea, the child should quickly close the discussion with another PPR response, or else the peer may talk the child into trouble!

9. Suggest a Better Idea

The "Better Mousetrap"

The child can quickly suggest something else to do, something without unpleasant consequences. A better idea can fill the void left by the child's refusal to get involved in the trouble. It can divert his friends, as well as him, from trouble, and they can all have fun, which was the original goal after all.

The better idea is phrased as an enthusiastic question-invitation: "How about (or, "Why don't we)_____instead." Or, "I've got a good idea! Let's go_____" ("see my new video game," "to my house for a snack," "walk my dog," "visit another friend," "ride bikes," "see what's on TV," etc.).

The child suggests the alternative with energy and enthusiasm and sweeps the peer along in his wake before the peer has a chance to think of reasons and ways to resist. For this technique to work successfully, it is *critical* that the child take *immediate* action to pursue the idea he suggested. The peer will usually follow.

"I've got a great idea. Let's _____."

10. Return the Challenge

When a peer is pressuring the child obstinately, perhaps even belligerently, the child may have to get tough. If avoiding the trouble won't work because the peer is determined to confront the child with it, then the child can throw the challenge back at the peer. He can get rid of the unwanted challenge by using one of the following PPR responses, which not only deflect the pressure but exert it on the peer.

There are many possible variations of this theme, so the child can pick what will work best in the specific situation. When ignoring, making jokes or excuses, or simply saying "no" won't work, it's probably time to return the challenge.

Following are three types of responses to challenges. They can be called on to reverse any type of peer pressure, but they are especially handy in dealing with negative, taunting peer challenges, such as being called a "chicken"; being asked accusingly, "Aren't you my friend?"; or being verbally threatened.

The most common mistake that children make when confronted by such challenges is to act self-defensive. By doing so, they defend themselves according to the *peer's* terms, instead of their own. This simply makes them vulnerable to further attack.

When a child answers "Are you chicken?" by saying something like "I am not," of course the peer's next response is something like, "Then prove it!" This backs the child right into a corner with no easy way out. Sometimes, if the child tries to deny names he's being called or tries to slink away from a peer or group ganging up on him, he may find that the peer or group follow him and continue to taunt.

The following are samples of effective alternatives:

- "Like Water off My Back"
- "The Joke's on You"
- "Tossing Back the 'Hot Potato'"

Return the Challenge

"Like Water off My Back"

The child says no to something, and the peer challenges, "What's the matter? Afraid?"

The child's response: "Yeah, I am. So what? Anybody smart would be." Or, "Thanks. I'm glad you noticed. I'm so proud of it." Or simply, "Yes."

He just blows it off, lets it roll "like water off a duck's back," without getting upset. What does this tell the peer? It tells the peer that the child is smart, self-confident, and secure; that he's not open to manipulation; that he believes in himself; and that the peer isn't going to shake his self-belief by attacking his self-image.

The child doesn't consider these challenges a put-down of himself, because he knows he's being sensibly cautious. He doesn't internalize the friend's comment. The peer won't continue to try to control him with what has proven to be an ineffective weapon.

Return the Challenge

"The Joke's on You"

When peers are saying ugly things about a child, often in front of other peers to embarrass her, they can be deadly accurate with their hurtful "jokes." The child can turn the tables by refusing to be wounded by the serious side; she only responds to the superficial side—the "joking"—by "joking" back.

For example, she is called a chicken, and she makes an exaggerated, sarcastic clucking noise as she **walks away** from the scene. She may even add a flutter of hands under her armpits, à la chicken wings, for artistic effect! She is communicating: "You're not worth taking seriously right now. But at least you're good for a laugh. I don't mind using your material to entertain the crowd. I win this round."

There are other verbal "joking" responses to taunts of "chicken," such as:

> "Hey, it takes one to know one." (Said with a laugh; otherwise it can start a fight.)
>
> "I'd rather be a chicken than a dead duck."
>
> "If I'm the chicken, then you're the egg."
>
> "I'd rather be a chicken than a 'jail bird.'"
>
> "Sticks and stones . . . " (an elementary-age standby)
>
> "I'm rubber, you're glue . . . " (another for the young ones to recite)
>
> "I feel like chicken tonight!" (Sing it like on the television commercial!)

"Chicken!"

"If I'm the chicken, then you're the egg!"

Return the Challenge

"Tossing Back the 'Hot Potato'"

This PPR response is used to send the peer's challenge, or "hot potato," back to her to handle. This puts the burden of the pressure back onto the pressuring peer. With sarcasm, the child refuses to be stung by her peers. She uses the peers' comments to sting them back, instead of allowing herself to be made to look foolish. And the chances are good the peer won't try it again with her! People who "dish it out" often can't stand retaliation. She has only played with *their* words, so she's not the one who comes out the villain of the situation.

When she's called a chicken, she answers: "Scared to do it yourself?"(Or if it's a group daring her, she could reply, "You mean you guys can't do this without me?")

If the peer answers, "No," she can wrap up with, "Then go ahead, but I think you know better." And she walks away.

If the peer answers, "I guess so," she follows up with a "Suggest a Better Idea" PPR response.

If the peer accuses, "I thought you were my friend," she replies:"Sure I am. What's that got to do with it?" Or, "Hey, if you're my friend . . .

> . . . you won't keep asking after I've told you 'no.'"

> . . . you'll stop trying to push me around."

> . . . you won't try to talk me into this."

> . . . you would get off my back!"

Or, "I *am* your friend, and that's why I'm not going to do this with you!"

"Chicken!"

"Scared to do it by yourself?"

How to Say It

You've read about what to say in a pressure situation. Now let's talk about how to say it. Appearance really does speak louder than words. The PPR responses are effective, but their effect can be enhanced by the delivery.

The child wants to make the PPR responses work so that the trouble is avoided now and won't return in the future. In addition to memorizing some of the phrases, the child must both **look** and **sound** in control and as if he means what he says.

Look the part. There are several forms of body language that communicate self-confidence, firmness of purpose, and control:

1. Good posture—a straight back and sitting, standing, or walking tall—communicates self-confidence.

2. In delivering most responses, the child should face the peer he's talking to and maintain eye contact.

3. The child should look proud, confident, and strong, even if he's not feeling that way. Putting on the act often creates a belief in the role. The child needs to look stronger than the pressuring peer. (Again body language is important. Fidgeting, looking down, shifting weight, or gesturing nervously makes the child appear unsure of himself or weak. The peer will sense the child's uncertainty and may pressure even harder.)

Sound off. In addition to looking strong, the child must sound as though he means what he says. Here are suggestions:

1. The child should speak in a firm, level, and steady voice, neither too high nor too soft, neither shouting nor mumbling. The voice should not quiver or end in a questioning tone unless the response is a question. (Although a number of the PPR responses are phrased as questions, they actually should be spoken as statements. The distinction is clear, as there is no question mark at the end of these responses. Example: "Why don't we_____ instead.")

2. There should be no weak terms or phrases in his comeback, such as "I *don't* think so," or "I *probably* shouldn't," or "I *don't* know." Replies of this kind, usually spoken in faintly whining tones, convey uncertainty and invite debate.

3. The child should apply the **30-Second Rule**: He needs to get out of the situation in 30 seconds or less. That's how he avoids getting trapped into staying on the topic and possibly being influenced by the peer into going along with the trouble. If the child takes too long to make his chosen PPR response and change the topic or leave the scene, the chances are increased that he will get drawn into the situation. Time gives the peer an opportunity to increase the pressure.

Remember: The 30-Second Rule is . . .

Get out of the peer pressure situation in 30 seconds or less.

4. He must avoid debate by refusing to give the peer an opportunity to persuade. He should say no, however phrased, no more than two times. After that second "no," he should use one of the PPR responses to end the discussion or walk away from the scene. For example, "I'm not going to talk about this anymore," or "I'm leaving," or the child just turns his back and leaves.

Don't forget: The Leave the Scene Rule is . . .

*Say "no," using any PPR response, no more than **twice** before you end the discussion and walk away.*

PPR in Action:

Examples of PPR Conversations

Now let's run through some sample conversations between peers to let you "experience" PPR in action. The action will cover the scenario of four different, but typical, peer pressure situations.

You will hear children use the three steps of the PPR skill: **Check Out the Scene, Make a Good Decision,** and **Act to Avoid Trouble**. These children are successfully avoiding painful consequences without losing their friends, and effectively safeguarding the respect and personal freedom that peer pressure could otherwise cost them.

You will notice that it often requires more than one PPR response to get out of a sticky situation with persistent peers.

PPR in Action #1

On their way home from school, two boys—Seth and Cedric—have stopped at a convenience store to buy soft drinks. They both have just enough money, and they're in the store selecting what type of soft drink they want.

Seth nudges Cedric and says, quietly and excitedly, **"Hey, I've got an idea."** (Cedric hears potential trouble in his friend's style of speech and puts himself on alert.) Seth continues, **"I'll give you the money for my drink. Go up and pay the clerk for our drinks and keep him busy. Then I'll get us both a candy bar. What kind of candy do you want?"**

Listening to his friend, Cedric has realized that his idea earns a "yes" from the **"Trouble?" Rule**. He decides that the risks aren't worth the gain. As he now looks over the selection of soft drinks, he replies, **"Hey, no, I'm not into stealing. I really don't want to"** ("Simply Say No").

Seth gets upset and retorts sharply, **"You chicken or something?"** Cedric responds thoughtfully, not challengingly, **"You scared to do it by yourself?"** ("Return the Challenge").

Seth hesitates a moment; then, reluctantly but with bravado, he answers, **"No-o-o."** Cedric comes back with a shrug, **"Go ahead, but I think you know better"** ("Return the Challenge"), and immediately turns his back to Seth and walks away ("Leave the Scene"). He saunters out of the store with the appearance of looking for something more interesting to do.

Cedric didn't hang around after that exchange because he had already said "no" twice, with "Simply Say No" and "Return the Challenge" responses. Had he stayed, he would have been inviting Seth to exert further peer pressure.

Another reason why it was better for Cedric to leave the store is that, in doing so, he gave Seth an easy way out of the situation. Barring that way out, even if Cedric's PPR responses had made an impression on Seth, giving him second thoughts about stealing the candy, he might have carried out the theft anyway, feeling that his self-image was on the line. With his friend watching him, Seth might have figured that he had no other way to "save face."

Of course, Cedric could have stayed and, ignoring Seth, gone up to the counter to buy his soft drink from the clerk. But the situation was too far along at that point, and Seth might have misinterpreted the move, thinking that it was Cedric's way of saying, "Let's get into trouble after all." Moreover, if Seth had stolen the candy and gotten caught while Cedric was still in the store, he probably would have shifted at least part of the blame onto Cedric's shoulders.

For those reasons, Cedric had to leave the store right then. He saved himself, and hopefully his friend Seth, from trouble. You may have noticed that Cedric had to use *three* PPR responses to work his way out of that particular peer pressure situation.

PPR in Action #2

A girl, Katy, is standing in front of her locker at school, getting books for her next class. Her girlfriend, Tiffany, rushes up and whispers to her: **"Hey, did you finish that math homework last night? I didn't have time to do mine, and I really need some help because it's important that I make a good grade on it. Would you please—*juuuust* this one time—loan your paper to me? I'll get it back to you before math class, I promise."**

Katy pretends to look for something in the bottom of her locker while she takes a few seconds to think. She answers "yes" to the **"Trouble?" Rule** questions and doesn't like the list of possible consequences. She's also a little upset that her friend would ask such a risky favor of her, although she understands that Tiffany is worried.

Katy responds in a friendly but complaining voice, **"Tiffany, I didn't even understand that math very well myself. You don't want my wrong answers; the teacher might notice that we copied. I'm going to try to look mine over before class and see if I can fix them up"** ("Make an Excuse"). **"Why don't you see if you can work on yours too, before math starts? You know, Tiffany, next time you have some problems, you can call me at home. We might be able to work on them a little over the phone and see if we can help each other figure out some of them"** ("Suggest a Better Idea"). **"Sorry,"** Katy adds with a rueful little smile. **"Gotta go"** ("Leave the Scene"). Katy hurries off to her next class.

Katy used *three* PPR responses to free herself from potential trouble while still maintaining her friendship with Tiffany.

PPR in Action #3

Shawn is visiting his good friend, John, overnight. They're in the rear of the house, in John's room, sitting around and listening to the stereo.

John suddenly suggests, **"Hey, I'm bored. Let's make some phone calls to some people we don't like and give them a hard time."**

Shawn knows that by doing this they would be breaking the law, and so he quickly answers "yes" to the **"Trouble?" Rule** questions. He decides that he will try to joke his friend out of the trouble, and replies, **"Yeah, and after that, let's place a call to the man in the moon!"** ("Make a Joke").

John doesn't back down. He retorts, **"Come on—we won't get caught. It's no big deal."**

Shawn answers, **"John, you're too nice a guy to do something that dumb. I don't want to have to visit you behind bars"** ("Flattery" and "Make a Joke"). He adds, **"I'm thirsty. Let's get something to drink,"** as he walks from John's room toward the kitchen ("Suggest a Better Idea" and "Leave the Scene"). John follows a minute later and finds his mother and Shawn having an interesting conversation. This seems like a lot more fun than making prank phone calls, and he joins in.

This PPR scene required quick thinking, since Shawn was at his friend's house for the night and it would have been awkward for him to leave the house after two "no" PPR responses.

PPR in Action #4

Special Note for the Young Child:

This scenario involves younger children, so the simpler terminology of **Too Smart for Trouble** will be used.

It's a beautiful day, and two young girls, Jennie and Mandy, are out riding their bikes. Both have their parents' permission to do so *only if* they stay in the neighborhood.

Suddenly Jennie yells enthusiastically to Mandy, **"Hey, Mandy, let's ride over to my friend Karen's house and see if she wants to ride bikes with us! She's only five blocks away."**

Mandy can tell by her friend's dramatic enthusiasm that she's receiving a sales pitch, and it only takes her a second to answer "yes" to the **"Trouble?" Rule** question of "Will It Make an Authority Angry?" She also quickly realizes that they will get in trouble for leaving the neighborhood if her parents, or Jennie's, decide to look for the girls for some reason or just notice they haven't seen or heard the girls in a while.

Mandy answers, **"Naah, that's too far away"** ("Simply Say No"). Jennie can interpret that "no" to mean that Mandy doesn't want to break her parents' rule, or she can interpret it as an excuse because Mandy isn't in the mood to go that far. It's fine if the reasons for the "no" are vague, as long as the "no" is firm! Vague reasons can be difficult to argue with.

After a little while, Jennie thinks of something else to suggest. **"How about if we go over to Amy's house? She's got a new game I'd like to see. I bet we can probably get over there and back real quick, before our parents ever miss us."**

Mandy is already on the alert for trouble, and it takes her even less time this second go-around to decide she doesn't want trouble. She's also getting a little tired of her friend not getting the hint, but she realizes Jennie is trying to think of fun and exciting things to do with their afternoon.

With that in mind, Mandy answers, **"Hey, my brother's got a game that I don't think you've seen yet. Why don't we go to my house and play with it? We can call Amy and see if her mom will bring her over, too. And she can bring her game"** ("Suggest a Better Idea").

Jennie answers, **"No, no. I really want to go over to Amy's house. That'll really be fun. I wanna go over there."**

Mandy's two **Too Smart for Trouble** "no" responses are used up. She states, **"No, I'm going to go home and play with my brother's game. Come on over if you want to"** ("Leave the Scene"). With a smile, she immediately turns her bike in the direction of home.

Surprise! This time, Jennie follows her, yelling, **"Okay, I guess I'll come too, and we'll just call Amy!"**

Mandy helped her friend as well as herself with her **Too Smart for Trouble** responses.

PPR in Action: It's Your Turn

Before turning to the next chapter, you may want to take a minute to try the PPR skill as you have learned it, to be sure you've mastered the basics of the three PPR steps.

Here's a sample of a negative peer pressure situation.

Nick is visiting his cousin Jay, whose parents have gone out to run a few errands, leaving them home with spaghetti to eat and a good video they want to watch. Jay asks Nick if he is thirsty, then adds, **"Hey, I've got a great idea. There's an open bottle of wine in the fridge. Let's have a glass. My parents will never miss it."**

- How does Nick notice the potential trouble?

  _____

  _____

- He identifies the pros and cons as:

  _____

  _____

- He decides to avoid trouble and makes a PPR response that fits the situation. He replies:

  _____

  _____

- Jay retorts, **"C'mon. We won't get caught. Besides, wine is good with Italian food."**

  Nick chooses a second PPR response:

  _____

  _____

- Jay jokingly taunts, **"You chicken or something?"**
  Nick states:

  _____

  _____

  and immediately leaves (or turns his back to do some
  thing else).

Which PPR responses did you choose? Perhaps a joking
line ("I never drink before I'm drunk," then reach for a soft
drink); or acting shocked ("Jay, if your parents came home
early and found us drinking, they would never let us see
each other again. I'm not going to risk losing you as a
friend"); or a true excuse ("Alcohol stinks, and tastes ter-
rible too. No way!"). Maybe you had other lines. It doesn't
matter which ones you choose as long as you comfortably
avoid the trouble.

Congratulations! You've done it. So can your child. Continue on, to prepare yourself to best convey this useful defensive skill to your child.

Chapter 3 outlines how to teach PPR one-on-one to your
child. Chapter 4 outlines how an educator or a professional
helper could teach it to a small group or class. Read whichever chapter is appropriate for you.

3. TEACHING PPR:

How a Parent Can Deliver the Skill

Here are some tips to help you receive the best possible results in teaching your child how to use the PPR skill. When you break teaching into manageable proportions, taking it step-by-successful-step, it's easier and not so overwhelming that you feel the need to procrastinate. Let's run through the five steps in teaching PPR, so you can then deliver this valuable skill to your child.

The 5 Steps in Teaching PPR to Your Child

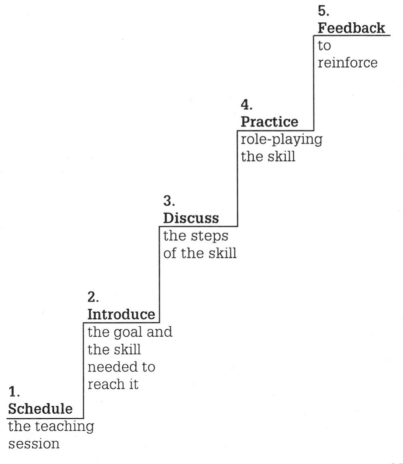

5.
Feedback
to
reinforce

4.
Practice
role-playing
the skill

3.
Discuss
the steps
of the skill

2.
Introduce
the goal and
the skill
needed to
reach it

1.
Schedule
the teaching
session

TEACHING STEP 1: SCHEDULE

With your child, select a day, time, and location for the PPR practice in advance, so that it fits into the child's schedule as well as your own. The appointment needs to be kept and not cancelled when something else comes up that conflicts with it.

The best location for practicing together is at home, in a room without distractions or interruptions such as telephone calls, TV and stereo noise, and people milling about. Sit quietly together in a comfortable, informal, and conversational setting that affords the privacy to speak and act freely.

Plan for the first session to be longer than the later, follow-up practice sessions. This longer first session allows you time to introduce the concept; the later sessions will just review, offer practice in, and reinforce the earlier material.

The first session should typically take between 30 and 45 minutes.

Starting the following week, 15-minute practices should be held once each week for the next four weeks.

After that first month of practice is completed, you can maintain practices at occasional "spot-check" intervals. Once a month is a minimum follow-up practice time for the next several months.

These "fire drill" practices are necessary to renew the child's enthusiasm, to practice responses the child may not have used or mastered yet, to check that the child is using the PPR-related skills, and to reinforce the correct usage of the three steps of the overall PPR skill. Your aim is for the skills to become so automatic to the child that little conscious thought is involved in their use. Many parents tell me that instead of arguing with the children about what radio station to listen to in the car, they turn off the radio and work on a few quick PPR practices!

During these later refresher practices, have the child review for you the three steps of the PPR skill, as well as the PPR responses he has learned thus far. If he has trouble rattling off various responses and can't do so without hesitation, then you can be sure that he's not using the PPR skill to his advantage with his peers. He's not delivering quick responses in pressure situations. He needs a few closely scheduled practices to get back into it, followed later, of course, by the "spot-check" practices.

PPR practice should be fit into the child's schedule as routinely as soccer practice, Scouts meetings, ballet lessons, band practice, homework, chores, and other responsibilities. It is every bit as important as any of those other activities. In fact, it will improve the quality of social interaction in many of those activities.

Teaching Step 2: Introduce

The parent's second step is to introduce the content of the session.

Begin that first session by introducing your child to the concept of "making your own decisions," or "being in control." The concept includes what it is to make decisions on your own, and why it's important to learn to handle those types of situations.

In the introductory session, you are not yet teaching the three-step PPR skill. Rather, you are stimulating the child to reflect on her own experiences with peer pressure, particularly those situations in which she found herself wondering how she could have handled matters better than she did. You are also giving her the message that you are going to teach her a three-step skill called "Peer Pressure Reversal" (or "Too Smart for Trouble" for the young ones), which will help her gain more control of her own decisions and get peers "off her back," as well as lead to fewer hassles from adults.

You are sparking her interest in the subject, as well as conveying excitement that there's a way to deal with a problem that no doubt has bothered her in the past. Hopefully it dawns on her that you, the parent, have something of importance to give her that she needs and wants to learn.

This is a very critical and important step, because you are trying to make the child aware that this skill—which you are going to discuss with her—can help her a great deal. In other words, there is something in it for her!

You could open the introduction with the mention that we all, no matter what our ages, experience situations in which others try to influence or pressure us. If you can, mention some peer pressure situations that you have experienced as an adult, as well as some that you experienced in your youth.

You also need to mention that peer pressure is almost always *verbal*. Rarely does anyone literally twist our arm to make us do something. The point is that sometimes we give in to pressure because we've allowed others to *persuade us* to act against our better instincts and best interests.

You are wise to make this point right away, before the child tries to catch you up by saying something like "No one forces me to do anything," or "My friends wouldn't make me do anything that I don't want to do." **That's correct: friends don't make your child do anything.** They do, however, sometimes suggest, encourage, and put verbal pressure on your child to do things she wouldn't ordinarily do.

This is a good time, too, to mention some of the examples in Chapter 2 of peer pressure lines frequently heard from friends, such as "We won't get caught," "If you were my friend . . .," and "Chicken?" Ask the child which group of peers are the most difficult to say no to, and expect some of the common answers: best friends, boyfriends, girlfriends, older kids (including siblings), and popular kids.

Ask the child why she thinks we all make poor decisions sometimes and go along with what someone suggests, even when we feel we shouldn't or we know it is wrong. Common answers are that the child wants to be accepted, to be liked, to fit in, or to be popular.

You need to agree that it's important to be liked and that we all want this for ourselves. Also, parents want this for their children. But we've got to remember that we can be popular and have friends *and still make our own good decisions*. That's basically what we're talking about: making our own good decisions.

The adult may want to comment that if a friend is *really* a friend, she won't stop liking a person because that person doesn't go along with all of her suggestions. You can ask, "If she's really a friend, will she drop you just because your ideas are different from hers?" The friend may pout or call her a name, but if she's a real friend she won't stay angry long. Ask your child to estimate how long she thinks her friend might stay mad; a few hours to one day is a typical answer.

You make the next point by asking this question: "If we let someone influence us and change our minds, who is in control of our thinking at that moment?" Obviously, the other person is. You need to ask the child, "Do you really want someone else to do your thinking for you? Do you feel that you have any friends who are so smart and who know you so well that they can do a better job than you at making your decisions? Should you let them make those decisions for you?" The sincere answer is, of course, "No."

You may want to point out to your child that if she doesn't go along with the friend's suggestion that they make trouble, the friend probably won't get into trouble by herself: she'll probably skip it or try to find a more passive accomplice elsewhere. Mentioning this to your child is worthwhile, as children like the idea of actually helping their friends.

Also mention the "internal" pressure that we sometimes put on ourselves. We *think* friends will consider us nerds if if we don't do as they wish. Or we *think* someone is staring at us because we haven't joined in. In fact, the other person may not even notice us or care what we do! Discuss with the child how easy it is for most of us to doubt ourselves and to be influenced without our friends even saying anything to us.

There are a few final optimistic comments you may want to make in your introduction. Your child enjoys both your trust and the privileges you accord her. She doesn't want to jeopardize those privileges by making poor decisions for herself. You know she wants to be a good decision-maker, that she's motivated to do what's best, and that she tries to be a winner.

With your introductory questions and comments, help your child feel comfortable with what she'll be learning from you. Give her the message that these skills are going to allow her to continue fitting in and being liked, but that it's also going to give her increased ability to handle pressure situations and to stay in control of her own decisions. And, most of all, if she uses PPR to handle trouble invitations, she will get more privileges because you trust her.

You can further explore the idea of peer pressure with the child by asking her to think of situations in which young people can get manipulated into going along with a friend or the crowd. Remember not to bring up actual past problems she has had. You don't want your child to feel interrogated. She'll probably mention situations she's seen or been involved in, and you don't need to let her see that you realize her examples are her own—unless she volunteers that extra detail.

As she shares with you some of the ways she sees children manipulated, she is visualizing peer pressure situations more accurately, especially in relation to herself. And her next desire will probably be to learn more about what she can do in such situations.

Allow your child to continue to talk about the situations and to work through them for as long as she needs to. This will let you in on how she is currently dealing with peer pressure. Be a good listener, and you'll learn how much help she needs.

Now that you have gotten her viewpoint and input, you both are better prepared to move on to the next important topic: the three steps of the PPR skill. Teaching Step 3, **Discuss**, will help you present the details of the PPR skill to your child in an enjoyable, highly effective way.

A Good Idea:

Prepare a chart of the three steps of the PPR skill, for use in Teaching Step 3. Or simply record the steps on a piece of paper or small chalkboard. Visual aids of this type will enhance your child's learning.

TEACHING STEP 3: DISCUSS

Next, after scheduling the teaching session and introducing the skill to your child, discuss it with him, so that he actively participates and becomes further involved in what he is learning. This will help him to assimilate the PPR concepts into his social repertoire. Your goal is to enable him to select and deliver a good PPR response in practice and actual situations.

You should discuss the three steps of the PPR skill with your child one at a time, point by point. If you have prepared a chart of the three steps, now is the time to use it. If you would like, use both a chart and a small chalkboard; then, as you work through the steps, reinforce important points by recording them on the chalkboard. Before you end the discussion, wipe the slate clean and hand the chalk to your child, suggesting that he now teach *you* the three steps. Whatever method you decide on, remember: Your child must be able to explain the PPR skill to you, clearly and fully, before you proceed to Teaching Step 4, **Practice.** Start your discussion of the three PPR skills with PPR Step 1. Do you remember it?

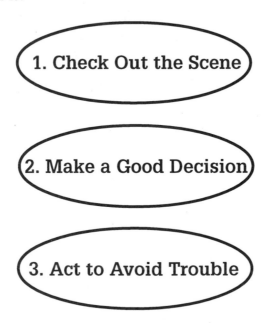

1. Check Out the Scene

2. Make a Good Decision

3. Act to Avoid Trouble

Discuss PPR Step 1: Check Out the Scene

Look and Listen. Ask the child what kids say or do differently when they are up to no good. Discuss opening lines that are frequently used to suggest trouble. Ask the child to try to talk you into doing something you both know is not allowed. This exercise often helps the child see how he's been led into trouble in the past. You're now opening his eyes to look—and look objectively—at a situation as he walks into it.

Apply the "Trouble?" Rule. Discuss the two questions of the **"Trouble?" Rule.** Pretend you are a peer, and make a trouble suggestion. Then ask the child whether it breaks a law or makes an authority angry. Do this a couple of times. Then switch, and let the child be the peer suggesting trouble.

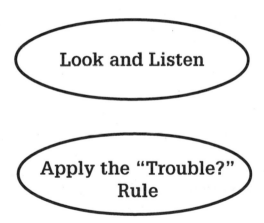

Look and Listen

Apply the "Trouble?" Rule

Discuss PPR Step 2: Make a Good Decision

Weigh Both Sides. Pick a trouble suggestion that the child has mentioned. Give her a piece of paper and a pencil; ask her to list all the good things that could happen if she went along with the friend, and then all the bad things. Ask her which one has more items: the "good things" list (pros) or the "bad things" list (cons)?

Acknowledge that the negative consequences *might* not happen, but remind her that there's always a chance they *will* happen, and that they often *do* occur. Ask her how many times she thinks she'd be lucky before her luck ran out and she was caught.

Discuss each of the negative consequences on her list, including how she would feel, and how she imagines her parents and teachers would feel, were that consequence to happen, and what the long-term results could be. Help her visualize those things actually occurring and their effect on her life. This intensifies the emotions—notably, the fear of consequences and the desire for adult and self-approval— which can help her decide against trouble in the future. This drill also trains her to think through action (cause) and result (effect).

When she acknowledges that she wouldn't want to go along with the trouble suggestion, review the pros and cons of what may happen when she refuses her friend. She needs to understand fully that every action, including good decision making, produces a result, and that she needs to commit herself to accepting the less severe price of telling a friend "no" and missing out on some fun, rather than pay the more painful price of the trouble's consequences.

For example, a "con" might be that her friend will be unhappy with her for a few minutes (but she can distract her friend and help her get over it). A "pro" would be that, meanwhile, she hasn't risked adult disapproval or loss of a privilege.

Decide: Stop or Go. Once she fully understands the pros and cons, she must choose whether to stop or to go. Then she needs to commit herself to that decision. If she chooses to go along with the trouble, she must be willing to face the unpleasant consequences. If she chooses to avoid the trouble, she needs to accept the loss of the fun and the necessity to make an effort to reverse the pressure.

She needs to be encouraged to avoid the trouble and commit to "I'm not going to do it. I don't want to risk the bad consequences." Strike a happy note by repeating the good things that will happen because she said "no" and proved that she is able to make her own positive decisions.

Point out that she will have to stand by her decision if a friend does not back down after the initial "no" and tries to persuade her to change her mind. Mention that it's perfectly normal to find it difficult, especially at first, to defend the initial "no." Doing so will become easier the more often she makes her own decisions when among friends. Assure her that she will learn how to avoid hurting her friends' feelings in such situations. Mention also that she will not lose the respect of her friends (and even gain more of it!) by sticking to her decisions.

Your child needs to be strong enough to stick with her decision to avoid trouble, and she will be better prepared to deal firmly with a peer pressure situation if she understands how it will feel if her friend pouts or continues to pressure her.

Weigh Both Sides

Decide: Stop or Go

Discuss PPR Step 3: Act to Avoid Trouble

What to Say. Ask your child to tell you what he currently says or does when he turns down a peer's trouble suggestion. He can probably name just a few things, such as "say no" or "leave." Explain that although these are great responses, they sometimes can be difficult to use if you are at someone's house, or in someone's car, or with a person whom you really like. Tell him that you are going to show him eight more ways to say no to his friends and still keep his friends.

Go through each of the 10 PPR responses and give examples (as outlined in Chapter 2, section "What to Say"). (**Special Note for the Young Child:** If you are teaching a young child, remember that you will be using the shortened list of responses.) Next, ask the child which response he likes the best and feels suits his personality. Generally, quieter children like the least verbal techniques the best, such as leaving the scene, ignoring the peer, and simply saying no. Class clowns will naturally prefer joking their way out of trouble. Talkative children like changing the subject and acting shocked.

In your own words, explain the responses and describe the situations in which these responses can be helpful. Before you actually set up a practice dialogue, let the child tell you what he understands each response to mean. Let him put the responses in his own words, too, but make sure that the words accomplish the set goal with as little antagonism of the peer as possible. Some children handle trouble by putting their friend down: "No, and you're stupid." It is okay to put the idea down, but not the friend.

The fewer "enemies" he creates while making his own decisions, the less trouble he will have with his peers, and the more likely he will be able to stick with the responses. Remember the old cavalry expression, "Try to get over heavy ground as lightly as possible." The lighter touch can usually accomplish the goal; the stronger responses are better used as self-defense in a situation with a very dominating or threatening peer. In other words, make sure the response is appropriate for the situation.

Avoid grimly lecturing on the subject and appearing paranoid about human nature. Laugh with the funny responses; use bigger-than-life drama to describe some of the responses. PPR can be taught in a lightweight and humorous way; it does not have to be confined to deadly serious lectures.

Above all, try to keep foremost in the child's mind that while some responses may be negative, they are used to change a negative situation into a positive one for both the child and the peer! The child is rescuing himself and the peer from trouble and negativism, and that's why sometimes he may have to "fight fire with fire."

How to Say It. Emphasize how important it is to make eye contact and to stand or sit tall (look confident!) when using any of the PPR responses. Make sure that your child knows and understands the **30-Second Rule**: *Get out of the peer pressure situation in 30 seconds or less.*

Also ensure that he understands the **Leave the Scene Rule:** Say "no," using any PPR response, no more that twice before you end the discussion and walk away.

Special Note for the Young Child:

When discussing the **30-Second Rule** with your child, mention that the length of 30 seconds is about the length of a television commercial.

Now that you have discussed the PPR skill, you and the child are ready to practice it.

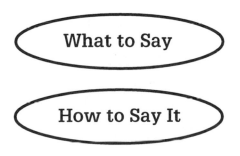

What to Say

How to Say It

TEACHING STEP 4: PRACTICE

Merely discussing the responses with the child will not produce results, no matter how much the child has participated in the discussion. The child may even insist that he knows the material and may be able to repeat it back to you right then and there. You will probably find, however, that his memory of the steps later will range from poor to non-existent. Not convinced? The average retention rate of auditory material for adults of average intelligence is 25 percent immediately after hearing it; 30 days later, if they haven't heard it repeated or haven't reviewed notes, the retention is down to a mere 2 percent.

Don't let the child pressure you into skipping practices; now *you* know some responses that you can use to deal with that pressure. Try to be a good example to your child in how to be strong and make positive decisions. Don't get into a debate about the matter; just state that you'll be holding these brief practice sessions and that they are here to stay for a while.

The child practices these skills by holding an actual conversation with you. This is role-playing. The adult plays "devil's advocate" by taking the role of a friend and using lines the pressuring peer might say to the child. Think of scenarios to practice in advance. Use pressure situations appropriate to your child's age. For reminders of typical situations, see the lists provided earlier in the guidebook (pages 42–43).

Begin with an element of surprise: Do not tell the child what your trouble-making idea is going to be. Do tell him, however, the location of the scene and the time of day if it is pertinent to the decision. This is more like real life, since peers who are planning to pressure a child never warn him about it.

Remember, **act out the scene** rather than just discuss it. And avoid using actual friends' names or specific past situations. Use realistic verbal and body language as you carry the scene through. If you would be standing during the real-life situation, such as in the school hall, then stand to practice its hypothetical counterpart.

Try to talk the child into breaking a rule, and really give it your best—his peers certainly will! His role is to play the child being victimized by peer pressure. He will need to use the three steps of the skill to (1) notice, (2) decide against, and (3) actually avoid the trouble.

Make practice a game, but insist on holding sessions according to the schedule.

PRACTICE

1. Checking Out the Scene

2. Making a Good Decision

3. Acting to Avoid Trouble

Now, let's complete the last of the five steps in teaching your child the PPR skill.

TEACHING STEP 5: FEEDBACK

At the end of the practice session, don't miss the opportunity to immediately reinforce a job well done, or to gently correct and try again a "performance" needing a little improvement. Most of our opportunities to praise or correct a child lack the advantage of immediate feedback. Right now you have a chance to follow the child's action promptly with your feedback, which will have greater impact.

Well Done!

When you reinforce a job well done, the child feels happy about her ability to use the PPR response and her progress in building a successful, competent, and strong self-image. This is a child who can go out into the world, battle peer pressure, and win.

As soon as you finish practicing one PPR response, praise the child's action. She needs to feel secure that you love her even when she fails, and you don't want your praise to send the message that you only love her when she does well. So, praise her *actions*, and be *specific* about them. For example: "Good job, Cathy. You noticed right away I was hinting at trouble. And you acted as though you meant it when you said, 'No thank you.' You sure walked away fast!"

Remember, her friends often make her feel good for following their ideas and "pulling something off" or "not getting caught." You want to make her feel good for making healthier, more positive decisions.

If at First You Don't Succeed . . .

What if your child didn't do such a good job on a practice response? If there was room for improvement, first acknowledge what she did well; then *gently quiz* her about what she forgot or didn't do well. Do not *tell* her what she did poorly—let her think about the matter and figure out the problem herself. If she needs your guidance, ask her what she would improve the next time she practices the response.

Don't supply an answer if she can't think of anything; simply get specific. Ask her whether she completely followed each of the PPR steps. For instance, did she do all the parts of PPR Step 1?

If she still doesn't realize what she missed, get more specific. Did she apply the **"Trouble?" Rule**? Or, did she follow the **Leave the Scene Rule** in PPR Step 3? If she doesn't respond, "Oh, yeah, I forgot to leave," you can ask her whether she ended the discussion and left the scene after her second "no" response, and so forth.

Tell her specifically what to improve only if she still can't remember what needs improvement.

Given any of the situations above, have your child practice the response again, so that it will be clear in her mind before she needs to use it in real life. And, of course, reinforce!

Before you begin teaching, let's review some "Do's and Don'ts" of teaching PPR.

Teaching "Do's"

Rehearse your teaching delivery before sitting down with the child. This ensures your success.

Maintain a positive attitude during the entire teaching and guiding process, including future reinforcement—even if you have a teenager who is rolling her eyes as you talk to her!

Use the phrases "decision making on your own," "being in control," "calling your shots," "being a winner," and so forth, to establish your theme.

Plan on teaching PPR to all children in the home. Teach one-on-one to maintain your control, apply examples appropriate for the child, and encourage the child's freedom of expression. Practice can be conducted together *if* your children are close in age *and* will keep to the task.

Tailor your vocabulary to the age of the child you're teaching.

Present peer-pressure-situation examples that are appropriate to the age of the child you're teaching.

Present all three steps of the PPR skill.

Present the simplified "Too Smart for Trouble" version to children in grades K through 4.

Involve the child in positive discussions throughout your presentation of the PPR skill.

Follow through on all of the practices described to ensure the child's mastery of the skill. Most children like the practices, but if your child doesn't, you must practice anyway!

Teaching "Don'ts"

Don't give this guidebook to a child to read. It is written for adults. (See Chapter 2 for a comprehensive list of PPR-related books written for young people.)

Don't single out only one child in a family to be taught PPR.

Don't procrastinate teaching this to your child. She may need it tomorrow!

Don't teach PPR to the child as a form of discipline for misbehavior. That would make this positive subject negative from the child's perspective.

Don't speak in a moralizing, lecturing, critical, or negative manner.

Don't use real friends' names during the introductory discussion or the role-playing practices.

Don't bring up past negative experiences during your teaching process.

Don't react to a child's pressure on you to drop future practices. She may, for example, try to convince you that she has mastered the material when it is evident she hasn't.

Don't doubt your ability to teach this to your child, thinking that you are not an "expert" on the subject.

TEACHING PPR: LIGHTS, CAMERA, ACTION

Now let's demonstrate three of the PPR teaching steps: **Introduce, Practice,** and **Feedback.** Three sample conversations follow—one from each of these steps. Together they illustrate how PPR can be conveyed to a child. They also will help you get a feeling for what constitutes a good flow of conversation between you and the child you are teaching.

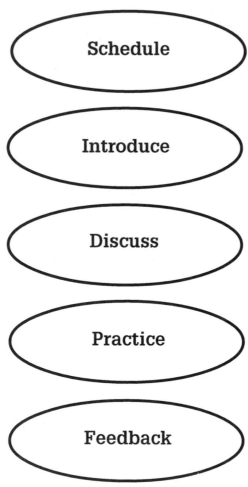

Schedule

Introduce

Discuss

Practice

Feedback

Three PPR Teaching Demonstrations

Demonstration: Teaching Step 2—Introduce

Parent: "Melissa, I'm glad we were able to schedule this special meeting. I want to spend a little time with you talking about making decisions. We all make lots of decisions every day. But I want to talk with you about a particular kind of decision that is the hardest for any of us to make—not small, routine, daily ones (like what to wear), or long-term, much-thought-out ones (like career choices), but rather those that have to be made quickly when we're with other people. Those are the hardest to make.

"We often make better decisions when we're alone than when we're with friends, since no one is there trying to influence our decisions and pressuring us to act in certain ways. This pressure is not really physical force, but verbal force. We've all heard people use lines such as 'Everyone's going,' 'Be cool,' and 'Chicken?' to try to talk us into trouble. What are some others you've heard?"

Melissa: "'If you were my friend, you'd do this with me.' 'We won't get caught.' 'It's no big deal.'"

Parent: "Melissa, sometimes can you say no to a friend's suggestion and make a better decision yourself?"

Melissa: "Sure, sometimes."

Parent: "I'm so proud of those good decisions. Are there times, though, when it is tough to say no?"

Melissa: "Yeah, there are."

Parent:	"What groups of young people are hardest to say no to?"
Melissa:	"Well, my best friend, and older kids too."
Parent:	"Yes, and what about popular kids and boyfriends?"
Melissa:	"Oh yeah!"
Parent:	"Why is it sometimes hard to say no to certain people?"
Melissa:	"I want people to like me."
Parent:	"We all want to be liked and be part of the crowd, no matter what our ages. If I don't go along with something a friend wants me to do and she 'drops' me, what kind of a friend was she?"
Melissa:	"Not really a good one."
Parent:	"I agree. Will a really good friend perhaps get mad?"
Melissa:	"Yes, but maybe not forever."
Parent:	"Are any of your friends so smart that they know you well enough to make your decisions for you?"
Melissa:	"No."
Parent:	"Nobody else can make *your* decisions correctly. In fact, if we let someone talk us into doing something we shouldn't, right at that moment the friend has controlled our thinking. Who do you want to do your thinking for you?"
Melissa:	"Me."
Parent:	"Of course. We all want to do our own thinking, so it's important to make good decisions. When you do, you earn more freedom from parents, teachers, and other adults to make your own choices.

	"When we make poor decisions, bad things generally happen as a result. Tell me some things that are likely to happen if you make a decision like that at **school**."
Melissa:	"I'd probably get low grades, or get sent to the office, or put on detention."
Parent:	"And those are loads of fun, right?! What happens when you make poor decisions at **home**?"
Melissa:	"*You* know. No TV, or I get grounded."
Parent:	"Yes, you lose privileges, as well as my trust. What happens if you make a poor decision while out with **friends**?"
Melissa:	"I could get hurt or arrested."
Parent:	"None of us wants to worry about any of those things. And when we make good decisions all the time, we don't have to worry! Also, when we make good decisions, often the friend doesn't go ahead with her idea, since she's afraid to act on it by herself. The only way she will risk getting caught is if she can find someone else who will risk it with her. Let's be winners rather than suckers!
	"How do you handle tough situations now when a friend suggests doing something wrong?"
Melissa:	"Oh, I don't know. I guess sometimes I say no, and sometimes I try to ignore the friend, but that's hard!"
Parent:	"Yes, it can be. I want to show you a way you can perhaps add to your two ways of handling trouble. Let's talk about it now."

Note: After completing this step, proceed to **Teaching Step 3, Discuss**, and present the three-step PPR skill.

Demonstration: Teaching Step 4—Practice

Parent: "Let's pretend I'm a friend in math class who sits next to you. The class is supposed to be quietly working on a problem. Let's act out how you would handle it when I say this to you."

(Pause)

"Melissa, pass this note to Sue."

Melissa keeps on with her project.

Parent: "Hey, Melissa, listen up. *Pass this note!*"

Melissa goes to the pencil sharpener and takes her time there. While she's gone, the friend gives up and gives the note to someone else to pass.

Demonstration: Teaching Step 5—Feedback

If the child is able to reverse the pressure in a practice situation, let her know what she did well and express your approval. For example, Melissa's actions in the scenario above merit this kind of feedback:

Parent: "You used two ways to handle trouble: You ignored it at first, and then you left. Quick thinking! I liked it!"

If the child isn't fully able to reverse the pressure in a practice situation, you can gently correct her and try again with feedback, such as in the following exchange. (This pressure situation involved the child saying no to a trouble suggestion on a playground.)

Parent: "I liked your 'no' answer. Did you remember all the ways to look when saying it?"

Melissa: "Oops, I bet I didn't look you right in the eye, did I?"

Parent: "That's right" (with an encouraging nod).

"Let's try it again, this time making eye contact."

Melissa tries again.

Parent: "Great! Now you've got it. I noticed that you looked very confident. That was awesome!"

The Action Continues

Now you've learned the basics of the PPR skill, and you've learned how to deliver it to your child. Are you eager to do so? If you anticipate no problems, go right ahead! Then after you've scheduled, introduced, discussed, and practiced a session with feedback, come back to the guidebook.

If you suspect you may have some problems, you'll want to read on before you start teaching, because the information ahead will help you control the child and get the PPR message across. However, unless you are a teacher, counselor, or other professional helper, skip the following chapter.

In Chapter 5, you'll brush up on the finer points of using praise to reinforce PPR behavior and to build the child's self-esteem. You'll learn techniques for effective discipline when the need arises, as well as easy but effective ways to distract your child from peer pressure and to dilute its intensity. This chapter will also clue you in on how to use organized, entertaining, and constructive activities, both individual-oriented and family-centered, to focus your child on what's important.

You'll learn, too, how you can better get to know your child's circle of friends and better influence her choice of new friends. And you'll find out how to take advantage of the parent network around you in order to control and reduce the negative peer pressure in your child's group.

4. TEACHING PPR:

Teaching Delivery for the Classroom

For those of you who will be teaching this material in small group settings, such as teachers, counselors, Scout leaders, or youth directors, this chapter will provide some tips on how to teach PPR and motivate students to use it. It is outlined in lesson-plan format.

It will take 45 to 50 minutes to deliver a thorough introduction and present each of the three PPR steps. If you have a group of 25 students, it will take another 45 to 50 minutes to involve all students in a role-play practice. If you do not have the nearly two hours you will need to teach this material in two sessions, then break the lesson plan into segments—15 minutes per day or week. Some people have even taught PPR as an eight-week course by presenting it in short blocks of time. Some schools have used the teen book, *How to Say No and Keep Your Friends*, or the children's book, *Too Smart for Trouble*, as a textbook supplement.

PPR skills training has been highly effective when taught in the classroom setting. In one school (Webb Middle School, Garland, TX) where I conducted a pre/post evaluation following training of 1,060 grade 6–8 students, the faculty, and over 50% of the parents, results were impressive. Based on referrals to the office, fighting decreased 75%, misbehavior on the bus went down 55%, not following directions declined 37.5%, skipping detention went down 4%, and disruptive activity decreased 17.7%. One student even went to the school counselor following my PPR presentation seeking help with her drug problem! Like any other subject or skill that you teach, however, PPR will require follow-up practices, discussion, and reinforcement.

PPR Lesson Plan

Goal

To teach young people to recognize negative peer pressure quickly, so they can think logically when in a peer pressure situation and take appropriate action to avoid trouble.

Materials Needed

- **Instructor**: Chalkboard

    Overhead projector/screen (if using the PPR teaching transparencies; see end of guidebook for details)

- **Students**: Pencils/pens and paper (for taking notes)

I. Introduction

Instructor's Notes

It is important that you lay the foundation for this material by discussing the frequency and intensity of negative peer pressure; otherwise, students will turn you off quickly. You must present the subject from *their* perspective, not yours.

A. "Today we're going to talk about making decisions. Decisions, choices—there are three kinds that we all have to make. One kind includes those daily decisions about what to wear, when you are going to do your homework, what to eat, and so forth. You've been making those everyday decisions for years and probably are good at them.

    "Then there are long-term decisions, which deal with matters such as college, marriage, and career. I hope you give a lot of thought to those, as they are very important.

"But we're going to talk about the third kind of decision that we all have to make. These decisions are especially difficult to make because friends often try to help you with them. Decisions of this kind are called peer pressure decisions."

B. "What is a peer?" (Someone close to your age.)

"Then peer pressure is what you feel when someone close to your age is trying to influence or persuade you. Can peer pressure ever be positive?" (Yes.)

"Give me some examples of good peer pressure." (Being encouraged to study, cheering a friend in competition, talking someone out of doing something dangerous.)

"Now give me some examples of negative peer pressure, such as things that people your age might ask you to do that could get you grounded, sent to the principal's office, hurt, or maybe even arrested." (Skipping school, copying homework, fighting, sneaking out, making prank phone calls, drinking alcohol or using other drugs, lying to your parents about where you are going, etc.)

C. "I want to tell you a few true stories about some nice young people much like all of you. However, these stories end on a bad note because someone didn't know how to handle negative peer pressure."

Instructor's Notes

Tell several true stories that you know about, or select several from Chapter 1 of this book, Chapter 1 of *How to Say No and Keep Your Friends*, or (for the younger child) from Chapter 2 of *Too Smart for Trouble*. The goal is to establish that even nice, smart, "good" kids can and do get influenced by peers; and that sometimes there are serious—even tragic—consequences when we don't do our own thinking.

Instructor's Notes (continued)

If the youth want to tell a true peer pressure story, let them do so if time allows. Remind them not to use actual people's names in the stories or talk about someone whom everyone knows, as few people want others to know about their poor decisions.

D. "What are some 'lines' that friends use on us when they want to get us to go along with the crowd? Let's review a few. I'll begin a line, then everybody help me finish it."

- "Come on. It'll be fun. We won't get _____." (caught)

- "It's no big _____." (deal)

- "I thought you were my _____." (friend)

- "If you were my friend, you'd _____." (do this)

- "Everybody's _____." (doing it)

- "Grow _____." (up)

- "Be _____." (cool)

- "Oh, you're just a big _____." (baby, chicken, wimp, nerd, geek, dork, etc.)

"Why do these peer pressure lines sometimes work? Why do we sometimes go along with our peers even though we know we shouldn't?" (Fear of losing the friend or being teased.)

"Let's look at that closer. If a friend asked you to do something wrong and then dropped you because you turned him or her down, what kind of friend would that be?" (A lousy one, or someone who wanted to be the boss.)

"Then what will a true friend—a real one—do when you don't go along with his or her dumb idea?" (Get mad.)

"Yes, but how long will that friend stay mad at you?" (Not long—generally a few hours to a day.)

"Big deal! Let's learn to live with that little bit of rejection, because if we don't, other people will be calling our shots. And I want *you* to be in control. To be winners!"

E. "So let's learn a skill called Peer Pressure Reversal. It will teach us more about how to say no and still be able to be cool and keep our friends at the same time. What groups of young people are the hardest to say no to?" (Best friend, older kids, popular youth, and boyfriend or girlfriend.)

"That's right. So we'll need lots of ways to put the pressure in reverse . . . to get away from the trouble . . . yet still be popular. What's in it for you if you learn and use Peer Pressure Reversal?" (More privileges, fewer child-parent arguments, less punishment, increase in people's trust, self-respect.)

"I guarantee you that if you actually use this skill, you'll get to do more things that you want to do and hear the word 'yes' more than 'no' from your parents and other adults. Why? Because they know you're too smart to be talked into trouble, and they know you're not going to talk anyone else into trouble. Peer Pressure Reversal has three steps. Let's learn them now."

II. Present

> **Instructor's Notes**
>
> Present each step and substep of Peer Pressure Reversal as outlined in Chapter 2. Not only *explain* what each step means, but also *demonstrate* each step. Be dramatic if you want. Have enthusiasm. This can be really fun to teach!

III. Exercise

> **Instructor's Notes**
>
> For students to learn this material, they must "practice what we've preached." So now is the time for all the students to take part in role-play skits. Some ideas for skits are listed on pages 42–43. Make the skits appropriate to the ages of your students as well as your locale.

A. For each skit, call two or four students to the front of the class. Split this small group in half. The students in one half of the group become "trouble-makers"—don't call them "bad kids"—and the others become the "decision-makers." *Whisper* a trouble idea to the trouble-makers. Then set the scenario by saying aloud where the skit takes place, and mention the time of day if pertinent to the decision.

B. When a skit is completed, have the students vote on the decision-makers with thumbs up (made good, quick decision plus kept friend); thumbs sideways (took too long, couldn't think of what to say, or put friend down—in other words, needs some improvement); or thumbs down (was talked into the trouble).

C. After the voting, ask: "Which of the 10 Peer Pressure Reversal responses did the decision-makers use?" Give feedback as needed, coach when needed (but not too quickly), and be positive about what they did well (rather than dwell on what they could have done better).

Exercise Demonstration

> **Instructor's Notes**
>
> Use the following as a guide to develop your exercise demonstrations of the PPR steps and substeps.

Teacher: "I need two girls for this skit. Okay, Debbie and LaKeesha. Debbie, you'll be the trouble-maker first. And LaKeesha, you'll play the part of the decision-maker. Remember, you want to try to get out of the trouble in 30 seconds or less and still keep Debbie as your friend."

(Teacher *whispers* to Debbie that she should try to borrow LaKeesha's math homework.)

"Okay, the skit takes place in the hall at school between classes. Lights . . . camera . . . action. Take one!"

Debbie: "LaKeesha, girl, I didn't do my math last night. Could I look at a few of your answers?"

LaKeesha: "No. How come you didn't do your homework?"

Debbie: "I was busy. Please . . . just this once."

LaKeesha: "No way! I'm not going to risk getting a zero."

Debbie: "We won't get caught. I thought you were my friend."

LaKeesha: "I am your friend. But I'm not going to cheat for you. If you don't understand the home-work, call me at home and we can discuss it. Hey, the bell's going to ring. I've got to get to class. See you later."

(LaKeesha walks off.)

121

Teacher: "Class, vote on how well you thought
LaKeesha handled the trouble."

(Teacher takes votes.)

"I agree. Thumbs up! Great job! Class,
which of the 10 Peer Pressure Reversal
responses did she use?"

(She simply said no, acted shocked, made an
excuse, suggested better ideas, and left the
scene.)

"Wow! LaKeesha used five of them. Sometimes it may take one response and sometimes it takes several to comfortably get out
of trouble."

Instructor's Notes

To save time, have the same students switch roles—
trouble-makers become the decision-makers, and
vice versa—and role-play a different peer pressure
situation. You want all students to practice being a
decision-maker. Save some nonverbal skits (e.g.,
passing a note, cheating during a test) to use with
those students who may be nervous in front of
groups. They can even remain seated for those skits,
and therefore will feel more comfortable participating.

Teacher: "Now, LaKeesha will become a trouble-
maker temporarily; and Debbie, we'll see if
you can handle a trouble situation."

(Teacher *whispers* to LaKeesha that she
should try to get Debbie to gossip about a
new girl named Trudy.)

"The location of this skit is the cafeteria, and
it is lunch time. Action!"

LaKeesha: "Have you met that new girl, Trudy?"

Debbie:	"Yeah. She's in my history class."
LaKeesha:	"Do you like her? I think she's stuck-up."
Debbie:	"She seemed okay to me. I think she's just lonely and doesn't know what to say."
LaKeesha:	"And her clothes are ridiculous! They look so cheap."
Debbie:	"LaKeesha, she may be wearing the best that her family can afford. Besides, clothes don't make who you are! Hey, what movie do you want to go to this weekend? Or would you rather go skating?"
LaKeesha:	"Let's see that new movie with Tom Cruise!"
Teacher:	"Fantastic! Class, vote on how well you think LaKeesha did."

(Teacher takes votes.)

"Look at all those thumbs-up! Students, which of the 10 Peer Pressure Reversal responses did she use?"

(She made an excuse, acted shocked, and changed the subject.)

Instructor's Notes

Now call a group of boys up to the front of the class, and set up a skit. For *most* of the skits, have boys role-play with boys, and girls with girls, because that is the way most peer pressure situations occur. For example, boys steal with other boys, and girls steal with other girls.

Depending on the age of your students, you may want to do a few age-appropriate boy-girl skits, such as leaving a school dance early to "walk around," getting into a liquor cabinet at a party, and riding around with someone of the opposite sex whom the young person just met.

IV. Summary

Instructor's Notes

Congratulate the students on their efforts, and summarize what they have learned. If you will be working with the students again, or if you see them regularly, mention that you will want to know how they used the PPR skill in real-life peer pressure situations. See the sample summary below.

Teacher: "You all did such a good job. Remember: Your friends don't *make* you do something that's wrong, they just try to convince you to do something that's wrong. But you've learned today there are a lot of ways to be in control, call your own shots, and handle any trouble that comes your way. What you've learned today will help not only you but your friends as well.

"We'll be talking more about Peer Pressure Reversal in the weeks ahead. The next time we talk about it, I want to know how you used it, because you'll probably need it within the next 24 hours!"

V. Follow-Up Ideas

To help the students retain what you have taught them and to trouble-shoot any problems they might have with it, here are some follow-up ideas that are appropriate to various class subjects.

1. Perform more skits, and be creative in thinking of peer pressure situations (e.g., guys in locker room "bragging" about how far they got with their girlfriends, co-workers trying to get others to punch their timecards so they can leave work early, stopping-up commode in school bathroom). Don't,

however, introduce any ideas that the students haven't yet thought of!

2. Use *How to Say No and Keep Your Friends* as a textbook, and have various students read sections of it to the class; then discuss.

3. Have students do a report on their most difficult peer pressure decision and whether or not they made a good decision.

4. Discuss how we sometimes pressure ourselves into going along with the crowd. We *think* others are looking at us with disdain, or we *feel* they think we are nerds, so we go along with the trouble even though they are not pressuring us to do so. Talk about where these self-doubts come from and what we can do to truly be more confident.

5. Discuss the effects of the media on our lives (e.g., glamorizing unhealthy things at times), and have students do a report on the topic or discuss it.

6. Ask students to do a collage of product advertisements (e.g., cigarette ads, clothing brand labels), that displays how such ads try to make us think that bright, beautiful people do certain things or wear certain brands.

7. Have students write, edit, direct, and act in a play about negative peer pressure (a semester project). Perform for the students' school or for another school.

8. Ask students to discuss "truth in advertising" and talk about what the alcohol and tobacco ads do not tell us. Have them write and demonstrate commercials for these products as the commercials should be (e.g., vomiting after drinking, coughing after smoking).

9. Several weeks after PPR training, ask students to discuss or write about the times when they used the PPR skill and how it worked for them.

10. Give students some hypothetical situations as examples of negative peer pressure that may occur when they are adults. Point out that we have peer pressure decisions to make all our lives, and have students discuss ways to handle these problems (e.g., beginning a family after marriage, owning status cars, drinking socially).

11. Describe some of the peer pressure decisions that you had to make when you were in school (if appropriate). They can learn from your examples.

5. REINFORCING PPR:

Maintaining Responsible Behavior and Emphasizing the Positive

As you teach the PPR skill and the child begins to make use of PPR in his or her social circles, you should reinforce the child's responsible behavior. This chapter gives you five practical ways to do so. If you are a parent, you can read this chapter with the intent of implementing or strengthening these skills in your own home. If you are a professional helper, you can read this chapter with the idea of sharing these skills with the parents of the young people with whom you work.

Why do you need to reinforce with these techniques? Reinforcing helps to ensure that you don't lose what you and the child have gained by learning the PPR skill.

These techniques help you encourage the child to the point where responsible decision making becomes a habit that continues into adulthood. By this process, you help to develop or increase positive attitudes among all family members—their attitude about themselves and each other.

Not only do these reinforcing techniques make life more pleasant for all family members by fostering feelings of caring, success, and self-esteem, but they also make life easier by reducing family troubles caused by poor decision making.

You may already use some of the techniques, such as praising and disciplining. The following suggestions show you ways to refine or strengthen your parenting methods and make them more effective.

Certain techniques may be new to you, such as how to organize activity to alleviate some of the peer pressure on the child, how to influence the child's choice of friends, and how to use "parent-power."

All of the techniques are common sense, attainable, and often very enjoyable and upbeat.

Most parents do not feel 100 percent secure about every aspect of their parenting. Here are practical ways to help you feel that you are backing up your child's reach for maturity to the best of your abilities.

129

The Five Reinforcing Techniques

1. **Encouraging the Positive.** The most effective way to praise. Builds self-esteem, confidence, and positive relationships.

2. **Disciplining Effectively.** When you need to discipline your child, and how to do it so that it is needed less often. Plus how to stop your child from pressuring others into trouble.

3. **Using Organized Activity to Dilute Peer Pressure.** Divert the child's attention from unwholesome activities, and reduce peer pressure, with organized individual activity. Build stronger family bonds and values with organized family activity.

4. **Influencing the Child's Choice of Friends.** Use this plan to get to know the child's friends, to influence their planned activities, and to help the child look realistically at his peers.

5. **Taking Advantage of Multi-Parental Networking.** Share the load, and get new ideas and support from parents of the other peers in the group. Start a parent group that will work for you, other parents, and the children.

All of these techniques are practical and in effective use by parents right now. When you invest your time and effort in the five reinforcing techniques, you find yourself with more time to enjoy, and less time wasted on your child's peer problems and ineffective ways of dealing with them. You may wonder how you ever got along without the techniques!

REINFORCING TECHNIQUE 1:
Encouraging the Positive

Once you have made the effort to master the PPR skill and to teach it to your child, encouraging the positive is essential support to maintain the ground you gained. Also, encouragement is critical to a good relationship between child and parent.

Why is encouragement so critical? Children need reinforcing praise and encouragement as much as they do food and shelter. It is a requirement for survival and health.

Your child's peers will often reinforce his poor decisions by praising and rewarding him for going along with their trouble-making suggestions and not getting caught. Your child relies on you to balance that negative pressure with praise for making healthy decisions. If you fail him, the burden rests on his young shoulders to resist negative pressure, which is rarely possible for a child.

Your verbalized praise expresses your loving approval, and it is one of the most powerful parenting skills at your command. Use it to reinforce responsible behavior in your child, and thereby help your child develop into a positive, happy, and successful individual.

Even the most effective parents (and other adults with whom the child has contact) often fail to praise the child as often or as directly as he needs it. You will probably find that you can identify with one or both of the two areas where we all typically fall short. The first: failing to praise when the child needs it; since good behavior is what's expected, we often take it for granted. The second: we may notice the child's good behavior but then praise with "put-down" praise; that is, with a moral or a lecture attached. We must become conscious of our shortcomings in this area, and give wholehearted praise when a child merits it.

Familiarity Breeds Contempt

The words *family* and *familiarity* are from the same root. The people with whom we live are the most familiar to us, and it is so easy to treat them casually, not affording them the consideration and respect we would give to mere strangers or acquaintances. It all comes down to our taking each other for granted. We don't mean to; our loved ones are the most important people in the world to us. But it happens nonetheless.

When we take the good in our homelife for granted, any negative behavior in the home shocks us and so gets our attention. We become irritated over it, and we comment on it. When good things happen, we feel satisfied and happy, but we often don't express this to the child because we are embarrassed at seeming sentimental. Or maybe we are just busy and never get around to it. But we rarely forget to express to the child when he has done a poor job or needs to make some major behavior improvement. Our sense of duty is usually strong enough for that. Of course it is important to correct negative behavior in our children; I've devoted a section in this chapter to structured discipline. The point here is that when a child does well, we need to reinforce the behavior with praise.

And it's true that children aren't the only ones who are taken for granted in families and who don't get enough verbal reinforcement. Children often take parents for granted. And spouses take each other for granted, as do bosses, employees, and friends. However, when these same people do something we don't like, we notice immediately.

In the full classrooms of today's schools, it's very easy for teachers to take the positive in children for granted, thus reinforcing the children's feelings that nobody notices their efforts. The teachers are often so busy with practical concerns—dealing with behavior problems, checking attendance, listening to announcements, grading papers, and, on top of it all, trying to teach the curriculum—that they don't always find the time to reinforce the children's efforts to do well. Children's peers aren't a good source of praise, either; they are usually struggling to compete with one another and rarely feel they can afford to be generous to others.

Therefore, parents need to double their emphasis on the good. We can't guarantee that children are getting any praise outside the home—and no matter how much they are getting elsewhere, it is not the tremendous amount they need.

When we adults don't get praise, most of us go through our day and carry out our responsibilities anyway, from an adult sense of duty and conscience, and a mature understanding of rewards and consequences. Obviously, children are different. Those who are not getting a significant amount of praise will act up or act out their needs in various ways to try to get some kind of attention.

When children act in a negative way in order to guarantee adult attention, it is often because that negative attention is more preferable to them than little or no attention at all. Here are some examples of acting-out behavior that you can often spot as a need for parental attention:

- The child talks too much in class, acts up, or is the class clown or bully.

- The child has vague aches, pains, and complaints: his head, tummy, or arm often hurts, for example. You have had the child examined, and nothing is physically wrong. Yet the child is constantly in the nurse's office at school or coming to you with something unidentified. This is a way to get some kind of attention: you have to take his temperature, talk with him for a few minutes, and so forth.

- The child asks for compliments frequently, saying things like "Am I really pretty?" and "Do you love me?" Questions such as these show the child's insecurity and lack of self-confidence and self-esteem. Such questions indicate that your child needs more reinforcement from you.

- The child shows you something she's proud of—a picture she drew or a test paper on which she did well—and shows you not once, but over and over again.

- The child refuses to accept praise, saying things such as "I don't like it" and "It's no big deal." These questions indicate that your child does not internalize good feelings.

133

The amount of praise that children need just to get by is completely astonishing. If they don't get it, they will take some sort of action—whether acceptable or not—to get attention of any kind from you or others. The more sincere praise your child receives, the happier you'll find yourself with the child!

"Put-Down" Praise

Failing to praise enough is a major parenting trap. Another is praise with a kick in it: We remember to praise, but in giving that praise we feel compelled to add something at the end that actually detracts from the praise—and that may even completely undermine it. We do not do this intentionally; we mean well and have only the highest motivations. It is not meant to discourage the child; in fact, we often think we are motivating and teaching with such praise. "Put-down" praise is voiced approval with an added statement intended to get someone to do a better job or to keep up the good work.

This "praise-kick" communicates that our praise is conditional, dependent on circumstances other than the issue of the moment: the good that was done. Conditional praise is disappointing and non-reinforcing to the recipient who did a good job and wants to hear that achievement praised without negativism. Even if we have injected the slightest bit of negativism into our praise, we haven't really praised the child: Praise is 100 percent positive. It focuses only on the moment and the good. It doesn't refer to yesterday or tomorrow. It calls attention only to what is happening right now.

Here are some examples of put-down praise: "You did a really good job on this, but . . .," or "Thanks for helping; it was nice not having to remind you." A simple reference to the past can be a discouraging word. "This is really a lot better than last Saturday's room cleaning. If you had done it this well last Saturday, you would have been allowed to go out and play a lot sooner. I hope you have learned from this."

A reference to the future can also detract from the praise. For example, your child brings home a good report card of all A's and B's. You praise your child, but then add, patting the child's back, "Keep up the good work. In fact, I bet if you studied just a little more, you could make all A's." Such conditional praise is bittersweet; the child deserves better.

The Benefits of Praise

Praise is a verbal report, support, and award. There are seven good reasons why it is important that you praise the child regularly and frequently. Let's take a look at them.

1. Repeated Good Behavior

You can use praise to encourage your child to repeat a good act or to continue acceptable behavior. By focusing on good behavior, you are encouraging it in general, because a child wants her parents' attention and will try to behave in a way that gets it for her. Reinforce positive behavior by giving the child positive attention for behaving well.

The average parent is pressed for time and may feel there's barely enough time to correct misbehavior, let alone to praise more often. Sometimes a child feels that she has her parents' *complete* attention only when she has done something wrong.

Even if you do praise your child often and give her positive attention, if you pay more attention to negative behavior, your child is probably going to exhibit *more* misbehavior. She may not discriminate between "good" and "bad" comments. The more attention she gets from her parents, the more she will repeat the behavior that netted her the greatest amount of attention, regardless of whether the attention was positive or negative. It's up to you to discriminate, by ensuring that your amount of positive attention outweighs the negative.

2. Appreciation of the Positive

If you start paying attention to how often you praise your child, then you'll pay more attention to your child's activities, and you'll likely gain a better appreciation of the positive in your child. Instead of only noticing your child's behavior when he does something unacceptable, you'll also notice it when he's at his best—and be impressed by all the *good* things he does!

Moreover, being praise-conscious not only makes you more aware of the child, but also makes the child more aware of you. And as you better appreciate your child, he will better appreciate you. The result? A deepening of respect for each other, as well as increased awareness of all the positive areas of your lives.

3. A More Positive Home Atmosphere

When you reinforce the good behavior, the proportion of your child's positive behavior increases; consequently, you need to devote less time to dealing with the negative and have more time to emphasize the positive. If you fail to fill that newly created free time with praise, you'll very likely find that the misbehavior level has risen again! Children aren't stupid, even though they're not always conscious of why they do things, and they sense when they are being cheated out of available attention.

A home and its family are all happier and more serene when attention is focused on the positive.

4. Expression of Love and Interest

When you give sincere praise to a child, you demonstrate your love in one of the most constructive ways that parents have at their disposal.

Regular praise provides the child with regular feedback, letting her know that despite all the difficult "learning times," you love and care about her and sustain a high level of interest in her. This expression of love and interest makes you both feel good. Sharing a moment with your child, and giving her a little praise, is a great way to begin the day— far better than the hurried, "griping" way that so many of us normally begin it.

5. Your Child's Better Self-Image

There are two areas of a child's self-image that you can strengthen: self-confidence and self-esteem. Regular praise gives regular positive feedback to the child, who wonders "How am I doing? Am I growing up okay? Do people like me?"

Self-confidence is belief in one's own judgment, decisions, ability, management, and strength. Children need self-confidence so they can attract friends and can manage their own small world as well as possible. Praising can reinforce children's self-confidence and help them increase their capability for handling negative peer pressure.

More importantly, children need to develop self-esteem. Self-esteem is respect for oneself: a belief in, and a sense of value for, one's own good motivations and behavior. A child who feels good about himself will have more inner strength and security to help him withstand the knocks of the sometimes harsh outside world. Encouragement for his efforts and praise for his successes are the tools you will use to build his self-esteem.

6. A Model of Good Habits

When you praise children, you are modeling a kindness and decency skill for them to learn. You are teaching them good habits—how to show consideration and appreciation for others on a regular basis. They learn the importance of including praise in conversations and interactions with other children—and with adults as well! They also subtly learn the importance of praise in parenting, for the day when they become parents themselves.

7. Ability to Tell Right from Wrong

Encouragement of the positive helps children, especially young ones, develop the ability to tell right from wrong. It may directly confirm the child's idea of good behavior (or provide a morale boost if that idea needs correcting); or it may simply make clearer the difference between the right way and the wrong way to behave. In either case, the child begins to associate right behavior with praise and good feelings, and is happier, as well as more self-confident, when making good behavioral choices.

When Do We Praise?

Praise should be indulged in at least once a day; of course, more often is better! Like taking a daily vitamin, giving praise requires only seconds—a small amount of time that produces wonderful results. At least once a day keeps you in the habit of noticing your child and keeps your child in the habit of thinking well of herself and positively about you and the world. Try to concentrate on increasing the amount of sincere praise you currently give. Remember: Every day, the positive comments you give to your children should outnumber any negative ones.

Where Do We Praise?

Praise can be used anywhere. Demonstrations of approval are unlike shows of affection. Children can sometimes be sensitive to *affection* in public; but *praise* in public, especially in front of family or peers, is almost always acceptable to him. It helps advertise his good qualities and reduces his natural need to brag about himself. Positive recognition is sweet; and before an audience, its impact is multiplied!

Putting It into Action

There are five steps to making a genuine and effective praise statement:

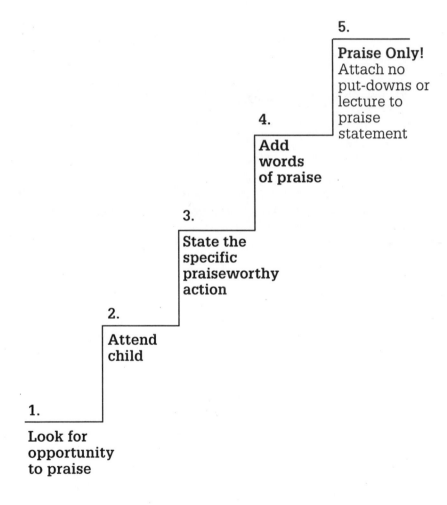

5.

Praise Only!
Attach no
put-downs or
lecture to
praise
statement

4.

**Add
words
of praise**

3.

**State the
specific
praiseworthy
action**

2.

**Attend
child**

1.

**Look for
opportunity
to praise**

Praise Step 1: Look for Opportunity to Praise

Pay attention to your child; notice good behavior; use her good acts as opportunities for praise; praise regularly and often, even if at first her good acts are only minor. Be especially alert to praise when the child tells you about a PPR situation she has just handled, or when you notice her trying to use the PPR skill.

At first the child may respond to you with shrugs or negative comments. Your praise may even be entirely ignored. Some children who are really down on themselves won't respond to praise, as they don't feel deserving of it. Their reaction to praise will improve as their resulting confidence builds over time. Don't give up on looking for opportunities to praise.

Please remember that the child may be so busy or preoccupied that she can't stop and smile or react. Or perhaps the child is not in the habit of receiving regular, positive praise from you and needs to become used to the praise and comfortable with responding. Be patient; you *will* get results from the most apparently indifferent child when you persevere! And try not to take it personally while you're waiting.

If your child is at a stage where, for whatever reason, she doesn't react or respond to praise, it may become difficult for you to keep up your efforts. You may think, "Oh, well, it's not doing much good," or, "Oh, she doesn't care." Don't think it! The problem simply may be a matter of time; or the praise may be working even now, but on the "inside" of the child. Although you may not see the good it's doing right away, you must have faith that it *is* doing good.

Praise Step 2: Attend Child

When you attend your child during praise, you are simply talking to him, looking at him, and making eye contact with him.

Stop what you are doing for a moment, and focus fully on your child. Square your body with his, maintain eye contact, lean forward slightly, and appear vitally interested as you state the praise.

And watch for the reaction. But remember, it may take time for your praise to elicit that little grin of response from your child.

Praise Step 3: State the Specific Praiseworthy Action

In your praise, you will want to state the specific action that you noticed and liked. A compliment is not praise, because it is vague and doesn't give the impact that praise does. "You're a good boy" or "You're a nice girl" doesn't carry the weight of a praise statement that points out *specifically* what you liked about the child's behavior.

However, a compliment can be a part of the praise statement: "It was very thoughtful (compliment) of you to go with your grandmother (action stated)."

The best way to get in the habit of making good praise statements to your child is to come up with a standard lead-in phrase. A favorite standard phrase is "I noticed that you_____." Another one is "I see that you_____."By using such phrases, you are telling her that you are observing her behavior, that you are interested in her, and that you recognize and appreciate her good behavior.

Be very specific about the praiseworthy action, whether it's tying her shoelaces, picking up her toys, making the bed, taking out the trash, writing down her homework assignments, or staying to the task while doing her assignments. Simple, yes; but effective.

The use of a standard lead-in phrase will help you develop your praise-giving into a regular, automatic habit. Everyone likes having a basic formula to fall back on, rather than needing to create from "scratch" every time. And without that support, you might be less inclined to praise regularly.

In dealing with young children, it is important to praise even small tasks. Remember, they may be big tasks to the child, involving great effort. With older children who are attempting a difficult task, it is good to praise attempts or steps toward the goal, even if the goal has yet to be attained.

Encouraging words can help your child believe that she can accomplish the task.

Despite the best intentions, if you don't make use of a standard lead-in phrase that states *what you see* (or *have seen, have noticed, have observed,* or the like), you'll tend to slide back into vague compliments. Those initial words force you to specify what the praiseworthy action is, and thus help you stay in the effective pattern of praise.

Praise Step 4: Add Words of Praise

Once you've stated the specific praiseworthy action, you need to add words of praise that will emphasize how pleased you are with your child. Here are some examples of effective words and phrases:

- "Wonderful!"
- "Good job!"
- "I appreciate it."
- "That helped me/her/him a lot."
- "I like it."
- "Thank you."
- "Great!"
- "Awesome!"

This is the time when we convey enthusiasm—when we put expression in our voices, smile at the child, nod, or do whatever feels right and encourages the child to respond. Positive touches—handshakes, a pat on the back, a "high-five," or a hug—may be in order as well.

Avoid giving praise in a monotone, "same as always" voice. The child may not hear your statement as praise, but rather as a general comment.

Also avoid being too wordy or "sugary," which may make the praise sound insincere or which may embarrass the child. Extra words of praise are like the whipped cream and cherry on a sundae: They are used sparingly to top it off!

145

Praise Step 5: Praise Only!

"That's nice, but . . ." Praise with a kick in it is extremely unhealthy. If the child's own parents can't praise without also "pinching" at him, how can he expect anyone else in the world to behave differently?

Sometimes you may feel tempted to insert a moral, or a lesson on improving other aspects of his behavior ("If you can do *this* so well, why can't you do *that* well?"). If you feel the urge to do so, try to resist it. It's destructive.

You may think you're only praising and not recognize put-downs within the praise. Here's a common school example: "Johnny, I noticed you were walking down the hall today. That's good. I appreciate your following the rules. I'm glad to see you're not running anymore." Everything was positive up to that last sentence. If you mention negative things in the praise, you've put a kick in it.

It isn't fair to draw the child to you with praise and then zap him with guilt: "I noticed how well you and the others are getting along. That's great! I wish you always could." That last sentence should have been left out. Sound familiar? Many parents give in to this technique in moments of weakness.

Here is another example. The child comes home with a report card. Dad looks at it and says, "Oh great. It's so good that you've brought up your grades. Now if you'll just keep studying as hard, you can make these good grades again." See how the praise ends as a lecture? You think you're praising. You think you're encouraging him to bigger and better things. Actually, you're moralizing. He'll feel that no matter what he does, you'll never be satisfied with what he has achieved. That can be entirely disheartening.

If you are not very pleased with the action but feel the child is trying to improve his behavior, be honest yet appreciative. Use phrases like these: "I appreciate all the effort you're putting out." "I can see that you feel good about how hard you're working on _____." "I noticed that you really put a lot of care into your English paper." "I see you're really trying to learn your vocabulary words. That's great!"

146

And so on. If you can't honestly praise the *results*, then praise the *effort*.

Praise Wrap-Up

When you're praising often and effectively, you can expect to see the benefits discussed earlier. Be patient for that to happen, especially with an older child. There are, of course, many other encouragement tools to add to your parent-child relationship, all of which can help you both: quiet times together, hugs, good-nights, cheery greetings, winks, individual talk-time with each child, and so forth. These all help to boost the effects of your praise.

You Get Some, Too

Pat yourself on the back for your daily efforts at praising. You need to remember to praise yourself too. You can get drained during the day, whether at work, in the community, or at home. It's important to recharge your positive battery so that you can replenish your energy for enthusiastic praising!

As your child develops awareness and praising skills, you will find yourself the surprised and pleased recipient of some appreciation and skillful praising. You can learn to be a good praise-recipient as well as praise-giver and show your child the same by your example. When your child (or anyone else) gives you praise, accept it with responses such as "Thank you" or "I sincerely appreciate your saying that." You are accepting the good feelings while being a role model on how to receive praise.

Praise Demonstration

NO PRAISE SPOKEN

The child comes home from school and makes a snack in the kitchen.

Mother: "How was school today?"

Susie: "Fine."

Mother: "Tell me about your day."

Susie: "Oh, Molly tried to borrow my math homework paper, and—"

Mother: (interrupting sharply) "You didn't give it to her, did you?" (Put-Down)

Susie: "Of course not!"

Mother: "Good. Maybe you're *finally* (Put-Down) learning something. You know you could have gotten caught if you had loaned it and risked a zero." (Lecture)

PRAISE SPOKEN

Same scene, but . . .

Mother: "Hi. How was school today?"

Susie: "Fine."

Mother: "Tell me something about your day."

Susie: "Oh, Molly tried to borrow my math homework to copy, but I didn't let her borrow it."

Mother: "You made a good decision. I'm proud of you." (Specific Praise)

Susie: "Yeah. I told her I wasn't sure of my answers myself, and the teacher might recognize our same mistakes."

Mother: "You acted by making a true excuse. That was quick thinking." (Specific Praise)

Susie: "Thanks."

148

REINFORCING TECHNIQUE 2:
Disciplining Effectively

Even though you have taught your child PPR, realistically you know that now and then he will still let a friend influence him to make a poor decision. It's important that at those times you immediately discipline your child. This demonstrates your serious intentions of expecting him to follow your rules and obey you. If you fall into the trap of frequent but lightweight verbal reprimands, reminders, or nagging, he will continue to misbehave.

Keep in mind that many peer pressure situations offer fun to the child, and he must be able to trust that you will take action (not just deal in words) when he disobeys.

Also, if you have a child you would describe as a "ringleader"—no one talks him into trouble, but he surely talks a lot of other kids into trouble—disciplining his inappropriate behavior is the most effective way to show him that it is not acceptable and will not be allowed to continue.

Discipline sounds negative. Saying no, setting limits, denial: These won't win you immediate popularity. Yet sometimes our children critically need the discipline we're tempted to avoid. When we provide it, we all win in the long run.

Some parents fear that discipline is negative and can be handled only in a negative way, and so they avoid it when it's needed. This chapter presents a neutral, constructive way of disciplining. The bottom line in parenting is, if you love your children, you will set limits to their behavior that they can rely on.

Many parents feel unsure of what is effective discipline or when to use disciplinary measures. Others who are on the right track can review this chapter for ideas on refining their skills.

Discipline should not be used continually, but when it is needed, it should be put into action calmly yet determinedly and in such a way that you really get your child's attention. Nagging or spanking do not get and keep your child's real attention. However, the right action—reasonably taking away something of importance to the child for a limited time—does get the child's attention. It makes the child understand the consequences of his behavior and teaches him not to repeat it.

Disciplinary measures should make a child "pay the consequences" for a set period of time, so that the next time he thinks about breaking the rule he says to himself, "No—I know what Mom (or Dad) will do."

Part of our dread at having to discipline our children is that, with ineffective discipline, we nag or find ourselves punishing the child over and over, more and more stringently, in a futile attempt to solve the problem. Ineffective discipline frustrates you, because your child repeats the behavior day after day and your efforts to modify that behavior constantly meet with failure. If you knew that you had a method of discipline that would get results quickly—reducing the recurrence of your child's troublesome behavior and the necessity for disciplining—wouldn't you feel more confident about applying such short-term discipline when it is necessary?

Let's think of discipline in positive terms. With effective discipline, you can be a more successful parent and your child will be happier. You'll be able to control his behavior and foster constructive habits, including good decision-making skills with peers. At the same time, you comfort your child by setting his limits; he will feel more secure in the stability of his world and his own place in it.

Children actually crave boundaries, even when they appear to fight those boundaries: They fear responsibility in an adult world, even while they strive to spread their wings and gain control of their lives. You *know* that both you and your child will be happier when the troubling behavior stops. Once you're in control in your home, the atmosphere will become positive and you won't need to discipline your child frequently. Effective discipline produces better behavior, whereas nagging or yelling harms your child's confidence, doesn't change the behavior, and gives you both a headache!

Discipline Don'ts

Before you can learn when, where, and how to discipline effectively, you need to review your current patterns of discipline to see if you are using any ineffective or counterproductive methods.

If you recognize yourself in some of these very common but futile methods, don't panic. You can change your pattern, and the transition is not difficult. Just make a mental note to work on eliminating ineffective discipline from your parenting and to replace it with the effective techniques you'll be given in this section.

Watch for and eliminate the following from your discipline:

- Feeling bad about making your child recognize the consequences of his behavior, feeling guilty about his behavior ("I'm a bad parent"), or being concerned about your "popularity" with the child

- Trying to be your child's best friend at the expense of being her responsible authority

- Letting your child's excuses ("I'm an innocent victim," or "I'm telling the truth, so I shouldn't be punished," or "I didn't know it was wrong," etc.) work to his advantage to get him off the hook

- Relying on discipline as your only parenting technique

- Disciplining in anger. Losing your temper either verbally or physically while disciplining models a kind of behavior that you don't want to see later in your child.

- Using unnecessarily strict discipline the first time a poor behavior occurs (unless you know that *the child* knows the seriousness of the act), and making your child endure consequences not yet set down as the rule

- Speaking negatively about the child ("You're so bad"); humiliating the child ("Even a baby could do better than you"); repeated spanking (this doesn't work; not only does it not last long enough to be a true form of discipline, but you are modeling violence, and your child is

151

likely to start picking on, and fighting with, weaker children); physical abuse (*never* warranted, no matter what the offense). Seek professional counseling if you use these disciplinary techniques, as they can seriously damage your child.

- Setting unreasonable rules, and/or setting consequences you can't monitor

- Choosing a consequence out of proportion to the misbehavior

- Setting a consequence with no clear beginning or ending, or for an inappropriate duration

- Disciplining in front of others

- Inconsistent discipline. Changing your mind about a rule usually results in the behavior being repeated. Examples of inconsistent discipline: "giving in"; one parent applying one type of punishment and the other negating it or applying another type; not disciplining at all; failing to follow through on your warning of punishment.

- Secretly rewarding the child with comfort after discipline from the other parent or an outside authority; changing the punishment originally stated, which teaches your child to manipulate you in order to get off punishment

- Giving up or quitting before giving effective discipline time to work. It may take time.

- Saying "Wait until your *father* (or *mother*) comes home." You appear weak and unable to make a decision. Plus you make the other parent the "bad guy."

- Not balancing discipline with praise. Forgetting to praise the good at the right times, and neglecting to reward with fun as well, will create an imbalance.

When to Discipline

Pay attention to your child and whether she is following your rules and observing common decency in behavior. Ignoring problem behavior does not make it go away; it's usually guaranteed to get *worse* for both you and the child!

Please hold your children accountable for their actions. My 25 years of experience in counseling families have led me to believe that this is the most serious problem in child-rearing today. It's heartbreaking to see the so very common occurrence of the parent "protecting" the child from the real world. True examples that I've seen on numerous occasions:

- The child steals and her parents blame the friend she was with (the friend was not physically forcing her to steal!).

- Parents are angry at a police officer for talking "too tough" to their underage child when he was taken into custody for possession of alcohol (the officer should be thanked for possibly saving the child's life!).

- The parent feels sorry for his crying child, who is upset because her name was put on the chalkboard in class (following several verbal warnings), and goes to the school to tell the teacher off (the parent should be concerned about why the child can't keep quiet so that she and others can learn).

It is far better for children to learn the consequences of poor behavior when they are young, because the world will be much harder on them when they are older.

When the child's misbehavior is minor and a first-time occurrence, it is appropriate to merely give a warning: "If it happens again, there will be a consequence." If the child asks how she will be disciplined, say, "I suggest you don't try to find out; you won't like it."

However, if the problem *is* a serious first-time misbehavior, then you must discipline the child so that she immediately experiences consequences and thus will avoid repeating the behavior.

When you are firm and consistent, your child will be able to use you as an excuse to avoid doing something wrong. You might overhear your child say, "I can't do that—my parents would kill me!" What great protection for her!

Be sure to discipline as close to the moment of misconduct as you can, so that the consequence is inextricable from the act. Don't wait for your spouse to come home; act quickly unless the misconduct is so serious that you need to discuss it with your spouse in order to determine the consequences. This exception should be kept to the rare instance, as you will appear weak to your child, which may prompt her to test your strength more often.

The need to act quickly means that the majority of disciplining will fall to whichever parent is usually at home and with the children. That parent will often feel like the "bad guy," so it is important that the other parent be supportive. If you are a single parent, you have to keep reminding yourself that you are strong enough to manage your child's discipline and that it's for her own good.

Where to Discipline

It can be most disconcerting when a child misbehaves in front of others. You may feel that he is embarrassing both himself and you. Misbehavior at home is disturbing, but in public it can upset you; it's as if your weaknesses and your child's immaturity are being displayed before the world.

At home, it is best to discipline in private, away from siblings. In public, attempt to take the child off to one side to talk to him or otherwise control his behavior.

At any time, whether in public or not, you should resist the temptation to take an angry swat at your child, to scream at him, or to lecture; but this is *especially* important when in front of others. Focus on getting the child to walk with you to a private place, where you then can discuss the problem.

Parents frequently say their child really acts up when a friend is over spending the night. If your child will not obey you, it is still best to discuss the matter with him in private as you follow through on taking whatever disciplinary measures are necessary (up to and including taking the visiting child home).

How to Discipline Effectively

There are four essential steps to effective discipline:

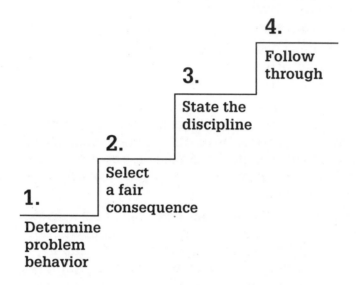

4.
Follow
through

3.
State the
discipline

2.
Select
a fair
consequence

1.
Determine
problem
behavior

The following suggestions will help you use these steps comfortably and constructively.

Discipline Step 1: Determine Problem Behavior

Problem behavior is destructive to the child, others, or both. Use your instincts about the child's act; don't react to her excuses, bribes, threats, complaints, or to your own resistance to discipline.

Your child needs your guidance and your follow-through until she is a mature adult and able to discipline herself. *Give the kid a break: Don't expect her to be a mature adult with the wisdom and willpower to discipline herself! Get her in the habit of self-discipline while she is young, by being her willpower for her.* Ensure that she experiences reasonable consequences for her behavior.

Time-Out

If the misbehavior is causing a near-crisis and straining your nerves to the limit, take or send the child to her room, if necessary, while you grab a moment to calm down and remind yourself of the effective discipline steps and guidelines. Take 15 minutes or less, if possible. Use that time to examine the child's behavior and to decide its level of seriousness.

As mentioned, try to discipline as close to the time of the misconduct as you can, before the consequence loses its relationship to the act. Only wait for your spouse to come home if the act is serious enough that you want to discuss the situation with him or her.

Examine the misbehavior:

- Is it a minor, first-time offense, which can be handled with merely a warning?

- Is it a first-time but serious offense (that the child recognizes as serious), which requires discipline?

- Is it a minor or a serious repeat offense, which requires discipline?

The behavior will fall into one of these three categories of action.

157

Discipline Step 2: Select a Fair Consequence

There are a number of good disciplinary measures that you can choose from, such as withdrawing a privilege or a luxury, taking away the child's free time, and retracting permission to attend a social event or to take part in a fun activity. More suggestions are provided later in this section.

Fair and effective discipline *does not* use physical abuse, lectures, nagging, or humiliation to punish the child, nor does it interfere with anything vital to the child's health or welfare: it simply takes away something the child enjoys. Decide which privilege to take away and for how long by objectively considering the misconduct.

"Too Soft," Said Goldilocks

Do you tend to be timid about selecting and administering a consequence? Try to remind yourself that you're not helping your child by teaching him that he can get away with misbehavior; he's sure to *continue* it. Also, remind yourself that although you won't be "popular" with your child at the moment of administering the discipline, he'll get over it.

The child may scream and cry and threaten, but try not to take it personally. You didn't choose to commit the act; he did, and he must learn the natural law of cause and effect. **Don't get emotionally involved** in the suffering.

The child may try the other tactic of cajoling and manipulating you by doing favors for you or reminding you of all the times he's been good. Don't fall into the trap of thinking that he's learned his lesson, so you don't need to discipline. If you've warned him once, or if it's a first-time but serious act, then you've got to follow through with a negative consequence; otherwise, he'll indeed learn his lesson—that he can charm his way out of trouble.

"Too Hard," Said Goldilocks

Do you tend to go overboard with your discipline by becoming irrational, saying things you don't mean, or enforcing outrageous consequences that don't fit the misconduct?

You may be reacting to a fear that your child is hopelessly irresponsible. You may see in the misbehavior all your careful parenting "going down the drain." You may feel that you need to appear strict and unreasonable to maintain obedience.

This can have very serious consequences for your child, especially an older one. Actually, you don't have to be controlled by those fears. Try to remind yourself that you now have a plan—an effective form of discipline that has been proven to work—if you can be patient, follow the steps consistently, and outlast your child's energy.

At first, you will need a few repetitions of consistent, fair discipline so that your child will begin to realize that you're going to be firm and reasonable in your disciplining. Don't overreact. You have a plan, and it works.

"Just Right" Discipline

There is a wide range of possibilities from which you can select the right form of discipline. Use your guidelines of "fitting the crime": not too heavy and not too light. You can be very creative, using different variations to make an impact on the child's constantly changing desires.

Remember that the consequence must fit the "crime." If the misconduct is minor, the consequence should appear minor to the child; a large violation requires a more serious consequence. In the same way, the consequence should fit the age of the child, differing according to the child's maturity level. Personalize the consequence to fit the individual child as well.

In some cases, you can choose a form of discipline that logically follows the offense, and take away from the child something directly connected to the misbehavior. For example, if the child rides his bicycle someplace off-limits, the logical consequence would be taking the bike away from him for a set time period.

Remember not to set rules you can't monitor. It's important that you only warn of and administer consequences that are possible for you to stay on top of as you follow through. Why? If you apply a consequence that a child can "wriggle" out of because you're not around or not able to enforce it, you've undermined your effective discipline plan.

So keep it to a consequence that you can monitor and ensure carrying through. You should only set consequences for times when you can see and check on your child. Better a smaller penalty that is definitely paid than a larger one that ends up being eventually forgotten.

The time limit? Two hours, one day, one week. *For an older child, the longest duration of any consequence should be two weeks.* If it goes on any longer than that, it loses impact and can have the reverse effect of what you want to achieve: it can make your child decide that you are unreasonable, irrational, with nothing to teach him, and therefore should be tuned out! Also, after two weeks you will probably start to get lax. If that happens, then your follow-through becomes weak, and you send your child the message "Don't worry about discipline from me; I won't really carry it out."

Several penalties can be issued at one time to draw the child's attention to one very serious misbehavior. These should still fall within the two-week maximum.

When parents "ground" a child or take away privileges "for a month," "until Christmas" (and it's only February!), or "for the rest of the school year," they undermine their *own* discipline. They become lax after a while, and as the child becomes justifiably frustrated at the long, unproductive discipline, the parents lose credibility.

At that point the child thinks, "I don't care about being good anymore. I can't do anything right anyway. Why should I be good between now and the end of the month? I'm already in the doghouse. I might as well do whatever I want, because I can't win anyway," and so on. That defeated attitude impairs self-confidence and the healthy motivation to be self-disciplined and responsible.

Consequence Suggestions

Take away something from the child that is important to her but not vital to her health and welfare. Firm but caring is your best attitude. (By all means, express your disapproval and concern with the misconduct, but be sure she can see that it's the act you dislike, not her!)

What are some examples of things to take away from, or ask of, the child as a consequence?

- Less or no TV time

- Loss of music (radio, stereo, CD player, etc.)

- Loss of favorite toy (although *not* the security blanket)

- No video games

- No play time/friend(s) over

- Isolation (**Unless** the child is a sleeper, reader, dreamer, or for another reason *wants* to be alone)

- Less or no driving privileges

- No allowance

- One-page, single-spaced report on "How I Could Have Made a Better Decision"

- "Yucky" work assignment (especially manual labor that's boring, or something extra you wouldn't normally ask the child's help with). Examples: clean car; wash windows, blinds, baseboards; rake backyard; clean attic, or tidy up basement.

- No favorite clothing item: boots, T-shirt, sneakers, jacket, favorite color of clothing, jewelry item, perfume, fingernail polish, and so on

- Loss of convenience devices, such as hair dryer, hot rollers, curling iron (**only** if the child is older, this is a repeat offense, and you need something extreme to get her attention; and **only** if the child will be inconvenienced and still look okay without the use. If the child would look truly awful, then you would be humiliating her, not disciplining her.)

- Can't close door to room (for an older child)
- Grounding: the child can't go to a friend's house; must stay home unless *you* take him out
- No telephone use
- Posters on wall removed
- Loss of an activity you usually share with the child (But don't punish the whole family if you select a group activity; the family goes to scheduled event as planned, but that child doesn't.)
- No money for treats at school
- Get up early on the weekend and have child run errands with you
- Have child pay for damages done, as well as apologize to those due an apology
- Earlier bedtime
- Time-out (for a younger child)
- *You* select the radio station when the family is in the car—"golden oldies" perhaps!

Discipline Step 3: State the Consequence

Be calm, firm, and brief. The briefer you are, the greater impact you will have on the child! State what he or she did. State that you didn't approve of the act (not the child). Explain that it hurts the child and others. State what the consequence will be and how long it will be enforced.

Avoid getting into lengthy discussions or lectures. You are not there to discuss matters with the child; you have made an adult decision. You are not going to change it, no matter how she tries to get around you. You do not need to get mad, either, because you're not discussing or weakening that decision. Try to keep the announcement to one sentence, stated unemotionally.

If the misbehavior is minor in nature and a first-time occurrence, then state: "It is wrong to do _____ , and I don't want you to do this again because _____ . This is the one and only warning that you will receive. Should this occur again, you will be disciplined. Please make a good decision the next time this happens."

If it's a repeat or serious misbehavior, then state: "Since you _____, then the consequence is _____." Period. You don't even need to remind her that you have warned her already. She remembers, and if she pretends she doesn't, that's just a technique to open a discussion and attempt to talk you out of your decision.

If you spend too much time stating the discipline, it's very likely she will try—with argument, flattery, or badgering—to talk you out of the discipline and the very limits she needs. Keeping your warnings and announcements of discipline short will help you avoid speaking negatively about the child; it will also help you avoid being manipulated.

Remember that nagging only contributes to a child's poor opinion of himself. He tends to believe the negative things you say about him and unconsciously fulfills them in the future, instead of stopping the behavior. He can lose faith in his self-control and his ability to achieve.

Avoid behavior that encourages your child to pull tantrums and to deal irrationally with problems that make him very angry. Not convinced? When you're screaming and yelling at your children, notice what they are doing: rolling their eyes, turning their heads, or even walking away, staring, glaring, or retreating into their own thoughts. They're trying to ignore you, as well as learning: "When you get mad, you blow your top." Children learn how to control their feelings by watching their parents do so. What's being modeled for the child, the child will inevitably follow.

Discipline Step 4: Follow-Through

Follow-through in discipline means two things: be consistent with the rules at every incident of misbehavior, and enforce the rules.

Without follow-through, the previous three steps are a waste of time and only serve to contribute to the erosion of your authority and control over your child. Follow-through requires consistency and watchfulness. Your child may fight you on the discipline with everything he has, but you must be stronger and persevere. You must outlast your child so that you have control and so that your child grows up to be responsible. Checking up on your child is not spying; it's being your child's self-discipline for him until he's a mature adult and capable of genuine self-discipline.

Inconsistency and lack of follow-through are serious problems in the discipline of children; in fact, in parenting in general. Children begin to think, "It's never as bad as they say it will be." The children unconsciously come to the conclusion that parents are unreliable people who don't follow through. Sometimes mothers are weak about follow-through. Culturally they are raised to be more sensitive and understanding in their role of homemaker, and as they often spend more time with the child than the father does, they are more open to seeing the child's point of view. This isn't always in the best interest of the child.

When you enforce a consequence, your child will view it as an invitation to battle—if you're at all hesitant. If you waver, the child feels almost compelled to try to assert his supremacy in the time-honored tradition of growing up. Don't issue that invitation: Appear firm and decisive even if you feel reluctant inside. Move quickly through the ordeal, so you don't have to maintain that pose for long. After some signs of success, you will begin to feel as firm as you appear.

If your child can read you like a book, that's good, as long as the book says, "I love you. I expect you to do your best. I mean business." When the child can depend upon what will happen when he does something wrong, he will think twice before doing something wrong. He will be less likely to do it.

165

Discipline: Wrap-Up

Inconsistent discipline creates a confused, unhappy, irresponsible child. Giving in on a rule results in repeated misbehavior. Follow-through should be as calm and rational as the warning or statement of discipline. You will enjoy the reward of seeing your child's misbehavior gradually disappear as she develops into a mature person who understands the consequences of her actions.

Don't allow yourself to lose patience with the discipline plan and quit before you've given it time to work. It is very likely to require several instances of discipline for each major behavior problem before your child becomes convinced of your consistency.

Lastly, for your own sanity, remember that the *child* decides to misbehave; you don't make that decision, and you should not punish *yourself* for it. You are responsible for seeing that she knows the limits, so that she will make the decision to improve. It works!

The following example will help you examine your parenting skills in terms of discipline. How does your child typically throw you off the track? Does he or she cry, beg, blame others, try to make you feel guilty? Why did you give in to your child the times that you did? How do you think you could have better managed the disciplinary process, now that you're aware of some of the pitfalls?

Effective Discipline Demonstration

No Discipline

Parent has taught the child PPR and the following week gets a note from the teacher that the child can't resist talking to friends in class. Parent says: "How could you? I've told you to just ignore your friends! I'm not sending you to school to talk! You'll never make anything of yourself if you don't do well in school" (Nagging, Lecturing, Negative Reinforcement).

Discipline

Same example, but parent says: "Laura, because you talked in class when you were supposed to be doing your work, and considering the fact that I've already warned you about doing that, your consequence is no TV for the next three days" (Discipline and Time Limit). "Later, I want you to be able to tell me which PPR action you should have used in class to handle that situation."

REINFORCING TECHNIQUE 3:

Using Organized Activity to Dilute Peer Pressure

Involving your child in activities—both family and individual—is a pleasant, effective way to boost the results of PPR. There are several rewards for the family as well.

PPR Boost

How does organized fun boost PPR behavior? In general, the child with a structured life is a child who is less out of control. Such a child spends much of his time in wholesome and constructive activities with family, other adult leaders, and peers. In this section are some "how to" suggestions for organizing activities so that your child enjoys the benefits of a structured childhood.

There are four specific reasons why organizing activity—both family and individual—for the child boosts PPR behavior:

1. The child stays busy and involved. Children tend to get into trouble when they're bored and looking for stimulation. The child with interesting, challenging, constructive, and planned fun doesn't have time for, or as much interest in, negative activities.

2. The child involved in healthy activities is more likely to meet healthy peers and to associate with them. Meeting and sharing free time with these peers leads to friendships.

3. The child who has fun in a wholesome way is a happier child. Happier children are more receptive to their parents.

4. The child who concentrates on an activity often becomes very competent at it, or at least feels good for having tried to participate in it rather than sitting on the sidelines. Constructive activities increase self-confidence and raise self-image.

Family Boost

The family benefits when its members feel responsible and happy, and organized activity can facilitate such feelings, increasing the quality of family life in several ways:

- With family activity, the family grows closer and stronger by opening communication and by building the friendly bonds of shared experiences.

- With family activity, each member of the family feels important to the entire family.

- With both individual and family activity, a pleasant lifestyle for all—with discipline outweighed by rest, relaxation, and fun—is maintained and enjoyed.

Why Me?

Why might you need this section? Don't you already try to do things as a family whenever possible? And can't children always find something fun to do with their free time?

In many homes, parents are not organizing enough activity for or with their children, which is the reason for this section. Parents may intend to do so, or they may even believe that they do so. However, if you closely examine the amount of family time you share, and the amount of time your child is looking for something to do, you may find that both you and your child could benefit from the suggestions here.

With these suggestions, you may find that you are able to fit in more quality family time. As for children finding fun on their own, they may not always choose well, and they often need adult ideas, logistics, or emotional support to arrive at better alternatives. Also, spontaneous fun does not always hold the guaranteed results of organized, regular fun.

Some children naturally gravitate toward a constructively active lifestyle. Other children gravitate toward the "thrills" of negative activity. And still other children gravitate toward no activity (become "couch potatoes"), often because they need confidence, guidance, or enthusiasm. In Chapter 1 of this book, we discussed how and why peer pressure is more intense in modern society. You may recall that one of the reasons is that we are usually too busy or too stressed-out and tired to organize wholesome activities for our children and group activities for our families. We mean well, but fall victim to procrastination, distraction, forgetfulness—any number of forces in ourselves and our lifestyle that compromise our priorities. And we all lose by having our priorities compromised.

To counteract this growing isolation, parents need to make a conscious effort to maintain positive communication within the family. Parents need to support their children by giving them regular individual challenges as well, to swing the balance of influence back toward healthy family values and away from the current influence of negative peer pressure.

Therefore, it is well worth it to give planned activities high priority in busy agendas. After all, what is of more importance to the parent than a close family that produces children who feel successful and who become happy and responsible adults?

This chapter will help you become more organized about scheduling activities for both your family's enjoyment and your child's individual fun. Being more organized will help you schedule fun more often. And some of the fresh ideas here may renew your enthusiasm and interest. Once you get it down to a system, scheduling fun activities becomes an easy habit rather than a major production.

Let's talk first about organizing family activity.

The Family Activity System

Let's call it FFA (Fun Family Activities). Using this family activity system will help you organize family activities in three major ways:

- By ensuring that organized family fun isn't left out of the busy schedule

- By cutting down on the griping and lack of participation that often result when the family is trying to decide on an activity and not everyone agrees with the final choice

- By keeping the entire family involved, regardless of their various ages

When Do We Play Together?

One activity involving the whole family should be planned each week in advance. To be effective, it should last at least 30 minutes. It may last much longer if desired, even an entire weekend. Frequent scheduling of family activities year-round is more important than investment in a lot of time for each activity, except for the occasional special event.

Don't wait for a financial windfall, either. The activity need not be costly. In fact, it is most effective when kept simple and requiring active participation; "paid-for" entertainment, which usually results in passive attendance, should not count as a family activity.

Where Do We Play Together?

The scheduled activity should be *planned* at home in a quiet place with everyone's active participation in the choosing and planning. TV and music off! Post a handy calendar or bulletin board on which the events can be noted for all to see. Be sure all family members are present during the selection of the activity, so that a firm date and time can be agreed upon.

The activity itself may be *carried out* anywhere in the world. It may be enjoyed in the home, or it may require a short drive to an event, or it may even involve an occasional distant vacation or educational trip.

Putting the FFA Plan into Action

There are five steps to carrying out the fun:

1. **"All Hands on Deck"**—Sit down with all family members present in a quiet place.

2. **"Brainstorm"**—Brainstorm to create, maintain, and add to a master list of activity ideas.

3. **"Eeny Meeny"**—Draw numbers, cards, or straws to decide the order of who chooses the weekly activities.

4. **"Planning Must Be Done in Advance"**—Choose the activity, plan its requirements, and set the time and date.

5. **"Follow Through on the Fun!"**—Follow through with the activity, and repeat the FFA process each week in the future.

FFA Step 1: "All Hands on Deck"

Getting all of the family members to sit down together may be the hardest part! Set the appointment in advance with each member. This establishes the importance of the meeting. Be flexible. If they're all busy, set the appointment for the last thing at night or the first thing in the morning. Do whatever it takes to get the process started.

You might find it convenient to plan the next activity at the conclusion of the present one. At that time, you are all together and feeling positive about spending time together.

FFA Step 2: "Brainstorm"

Start a master list of ideas for activities that the entire family will enjoy. When a new idea comes to you, write it down on the list *before you forget it!* Tell the group, "Okay, we're going to start doing family activities on a regular basis, which will be a big improvement over the irregular way that we've been doing them. We're going to do this once a week, and we're going to plan everything in advance. This can make our family stronger and happier, and I think we'll all enjoy it."

During this discussion, ask each family member to suggest ideas for the list of activities. In general, try to be sure that each member of the family is physically able or emotionally mature enough to participate in the activities and enjoy them. Each activity must involve family participation. If members can't talk together and share their experience during the activity, it's not one for the list unless you go somewhere together before or after the activity to talk about it.

If you have a toddler who can't talk yet or can't participate in something that the rest of the family enjoys, sometimes go ahead and plan that activity anyway. At other times, you may want to leave the child with a sitter (not an immediate family member) so the others can participate more fully, and so that the older children get more of the attention the "baby" often takes away from them. If you take the toddler, remember to bring something that will entertain him when his attention wanes.

As children advance from the toddler stage, it becomes more practical to give them a role in the activity, even though they are not able to fully participate. (For example, they could roll the dice and advance the counters in a board game.) Younger children are often perfectly happy to be functioning within the limits of their ability while being permitted to spend time with "the big guys."

Each activity should be reasonable, inexpensive, or free. Remember that the simple activities requiring the children's participation and creativity are usually a greater hit than the structured, costly entertainment provided by others.

There should be at least 20 activities listed. Why? Each child will feel his desires are well represented. The list will appear so enticing that everyone will want to keep it up week after week. And if unforeseen circumstances prevent the planned activity, there are many equally desirable choices on which to fall back.

Your List of Fun

The following offers many good ideas and can help stimulate even more for your list of fun. Be sure each family member contributes his or her ideas. The rare, elaborate outings can go on the list too, but be sure the family knows not to expect them weekly! Children need to be told that parents have veto power on choices that would be too costly or time-consuming to carry out. If you must veto such a choice, explain to the child why the choice would be difficult to manage, and ask her to make a second selection.

If a child picks an activity, date, and time that doesn't suit the limits of the family's time frame, remind the child that there is a time frame, review its limits with her, and encourage her to select a more suitable activity.

On the other hand, if you have a holiday coming up and everyone wants an extended activity, tell the children that now there's time for one of the longer outings, such as camping or taking a trip to visit relatives, and to feel free to select one!

Families come up with very creative ideas. Think about the talents and preferences of your family, and you will be creative too. Here are some ideas for fun that families have liked:

- Dinner with a theme (an ethnic feast, or a celebration of a holiday, either famous or little known). For such special FFA meals, little ones can make or draw decorations; others cook, plan music, and arrange lighting. Everyone might try to dress to suit the theme. Bring a book or magazine about the country or holiday to the table and discuss it.

175

- Jogging (the little ones can bike) through a park
- Boating
- Swimming
- Horseback riding
- Camping out—either backyard or farther—in tent, motor home, or cabin
- Resorts or amusement parks
- Home movies, slides, or album sharing
- Dinner theater
- A movie or live show, followed by refreshments and discussion
- Baseball or football game, with a tailgate lunch and talk time before and after
- Family dinner with "story swap," during which each member tells a story about a childhood experience, or even a recent one, that the others may not know about
- Badminton, croquet, volleyball
- *Password* or *Family Feud*-type team games, *Trivia*-type games
- Basketball shoot
- Miniature golf (I became good at this trying to compete with my father!)
- *Scrabble*, *Monopoly*, cards, *UNO*, and other home games (I improved my math when I was in elementary school by playing dominoes with my grandfather!)
- Picnics, cookouts—on beaches, in parks, or in backyard
- Bike riding
- Nature walks, identifying animals, trees, flowers, etc.
- Sing-along or storytelling

- Reading aloud from a favorite book (and if desired, acting it out)
- Tubing down a river, rafting, canoeing
- Kickball
- Jigsaw puzzle (This was a rainy-day favorite when I was a child.)
- State parks
- State fairs (The famous State Fair of Texas was eagerly anticipated every year when I was a girl. And my mother remembers when she was younger and saved money for a year so she could go.)
- Museums
- Boat shows
- Jacks, yo-yos, hopscotch, hide-and-seek, jump rope
- Pick-up sticks (jackstraws)
- Magic tricks
- Ice skating, roller skating, rollerblading
- Family aid project (for needy families)
- Backyard building: treehouse, birdhouse, doghouse, swings, fort, sandbox
- Animal or pet grooming or training
- Garden plots: vegetable or flower
- Musical jam session (if you can all sing or play)
- Window-shopping
- Garage sale (Have one or go to one.)
- Money-making project to pay for a fun outing
- Planting a tree (Discuss how that helps the environment.)
- Making doll clothes, toy furniture, model kits, etc.
- Berry picking
- Feeding ducks, pigeons

- Go-carting, skateboarding
- Neighborhood holiday-decorations contest
- Backyard dancercise, or playground playing
- Walking the dog; walking to church, store, a snack place, a movie, etc.
- Charcoal or colored-chalk sketching (For example, create funny or serious family portraits; then compare and enjoy them. Hang them in your house, or perhaps even give them to the relatives.)
- Crafts project (Make Christmas cards, valentines, personalized stationery, gifts, holiday or home decoration, etc.)
- Baking bread or cookies
- Taking a drive through the country or to the city (My family used to drive around Lake Texoma every Sunday afternoon.)
- Charades: acting out book or movie titles
- A "now a word from our sponsor" project, in which each family member writes and acts out a one-minute commercial about him or herself
- Recycling project
- Volunteering to help the local animal-welfare agency (Exercise the animals or donate food/toys for them.)

And whatever else you like to do! Send me your list!

FFA Step 3: "Eeny Meeny"

The parent chooses a simple, objective way to decide who selects each week's activity. This will cut down on arguments and competition.

Drawing straws, cards, numbers, or the like is popular and quick. One example: Cut a slip of paper for each family member; number the paper slips sequentially (1,2,3, and so on) and put them in a bowl; then have each family member draw one. Write down the order of the names, and use that order as your permanent rotation of decision. The person whose turn it is picks that week's activity from the list.

FFA Step 4: "Planning Must Be Done in Advance"

You must plan ahead. If you do not, then the activity may not happen as planned and may be missed altogether. Plan ahead one week at a time. Don't project ahead by two or three weeks.

Encourage the child who has chosen the next week's activity to lead the planning. Ask what day and starting time would be best for everyone. When discussing the activity with everyone in the family, suggest one or two days and times that you feel will be practical. The day and time can vary from week to week, but should be set in advance; if not, you'll have difficulty bringing about the plan.

Or, if it is practical for your family situation, choose one night or day of the week and establish a regular "family evening" or "family day." This plan is predictable, easy to remember, and all family members can avoid making conflicting commitments and wasting everyone's time rescheduling.

Discuss whether any advance preparation is required (purchases, errands, chores, and so forth). If any is needed, every family member must help, so plan how you'll divide up the jobs. Everyone has a pre-assigned task. Mom or Dad should not end up with all the work; otherwise it becomes a Mom or Dad activity, and the family is not interacting, which is, after all, the purpose of a Fun Family Activity.

Remember, delegate responsibility. Example: picnic in the park. Mom makes the meal. Dad loads and unloads car. Jill sets the meal out and fixes drinks. Johnny cleans up and puts things away. And so forth.

FFA Step 5: "Follow Through on the Fun!"

Make sure the children know from the very beginning that there are two basic rules: (1) no griping, and (2) everyone participates. Period. This is not a choice; it's a requirement for all members of the family. Siblings need to learn to be fair, to take turns, and to enter into others' activities with enthusiastic participation, just as they will want the family to do for their own choices. The no-griping rule goes for parents, too!

If you have an older child who says, "I'm not going," you make it clear to him that he is. Explain that you will try to make sure that you don't go anyplace where he'll feel embarrassed about interacting with the family. For example, date night at your local movie theater would not be a good choice if you have teenagers. As you know, it's not cool to go to the movies on weekends with one's parents! If a younger child chooses a juvenile activity, it can usually be done at home.

With some older teenagers, you may need to use your disciplining techniques to enforce the family rule of participation. Eventually you won't need to use discipline to enforce participation in outings, because the child will enjoy the fun and wholeheartedly participate in it. Anticipation of his turn to select an activity makes agreeing with the others' choices—which he may not enjoy as much—more worthwhile.

When you are disciplining a child and enforcing participation, don't say anything to him when you reach the destination for the activity. Everybody piles out of the car and ignores him. He'll probably trail along or sit in the car pouting until the outing is over, or watch from the "sidelines." This usually occurs only one time. If he joins the family in the activity, he will probably be surly or try to spoil the outing. Try to avoid letting him know when he is bothering others, as he is trying to accomplish upsetting the activity he is rebelling against. Achieving his cooperation and friendly participation may take longer than one outing, but eventually he will adjust.

No friends are to be involved in this weekly FFA. It's family time: time to get reacquainted and forge stronger bonds, not the time to be busy interacting with peers and to become distracted from the family goals.

This, of course, does not mean that you can never enjoy fun activities as a family with other relatives and friends. On the contrary, the more you do that, the more your family will think of the family as something they enjoy being part of and something in which the fun outweighs the discipline. However, for your routine, weekly FFA, maintaining "immediate family only" as a rule produces the desirable results.

Now that you have established the system, repeat it the next week and the next. You are the initiator of the FFA planning meeting activity each week. Don't leave it up to the kids even once. If you really can't be there (are ill, or will be out of town), then postpone it. You must always be the leader. Make it a priority. One of the saddest questions I ever had to answer following an FFA workshop was raised by an 11-year-old boy. He asked, "What should I do after a few weeks go by and my parents are too busy to keep doing the family activities?" His mother looked at him, with tears in her eyes, and promised that this would be the Number One priority in their family. I hope she kept that promise. I hope that you do too!

If you work in an office, mark the dates of the planning meeting and activity right on your office calendar, scheduling these priorities in big bold letters. Write them in your appointment book—in ink. The *other* appointments are not with the most important people in your life! If you have planned ahead but your work schedule changes, *immediately* reschedule the FFA. Otherwise you'll say, "We can just postpone it until next week," and in a blink, two or three weeks will go by and your family won't have had any time together as a family; you'll lose momentum and get out of the habit of relaxing and sharing.

Activity: Wrap-up

The results of regular family fun can be dramatic. For instance, take the case of two daughters—ages 14 and 16—who had not gotten along well with each other in years. The younger one excelled at making high grades and playing music, which made the older daughter very jealous. They didn't talk to each other, they didn't share anything, they had no friends in common, and they argued when they did interact. I asked the parents to start organizing family activities. The parents looked at me like I was crazy as the girls both set up a howl. The parents persevered in the face of their wails and complaints. One daughter always tried to spoil the other's fun, but she was ignored.

Whenever their parents took them on an outing, the girls sat in the back seat of the car, and for the first few FFAs they were fairly silent. Then they began to talk to each other, chatting about this and that. After a while the parents noticed that the daughters were also talking together at home after school. They began to truly share their lives, chatting like friends—something they hadn't done since they were little girls. Summer came, and they started sunbathing together. Every now and then they went somewhere together on what was not a family activity. The family outing program was *solely* responsible for beginning the process of drawing this family closer together.

The father of this family always chose going out to dinner for his FFA turn. He made it intriguing and fun. He wouldn't tell the others where they were going, but he'd tell them what dress was appropriate, and he'd drop clues about the place. Whoever guessed the location got to order a dessert for all four to share. They all began looking forward to it.

That family talks about the problems they used to have and can even chuckle a bit about them, since those problems are now in the past!

Just remember that this 30-minute or so period each week is one of the most important half hours in your week in terms of rewards. If you work FFA into the family schedule, you'll enjoy the rewards year-round!

Using Organized Activity Demonstration #1

POOR FFA PLANNING

A conversation in the kitchen:

Mother: "Let's do our family activity tonight after dinner." (No pre-planning)

Shannon: "I was going over to Alexander's house to study. I don't have time tonight." (Entire family won't be present)

Scott: "Please—let's do it tonight. I'm in the mood to play dominoes. That's a lot of fun!" (Out of turn on weekly selection)

Father: "I'm busy too. Maybe another time. Besides, I hate dominoes." (Griping; lack of support and participation)

Using Organized Activity Demonstration #2

GOOD FFA PLANNING

Conversation after completing one FFA:

Mother: "That was fun! I enjoyed being with all of you." (Supporting FFA)

Father: "Me too. Let's plan our next week's family activity now while we're all together, so we can fit it into our schedules. Would Thursday evening or Sunday be best for everyone?" (Support and participation)

Shannon: "Sunday afternoon would be best for me." (Support and participation)

Mother: "Is that good for everyone?" (Pre-planning and participation)

Family: "Yes."

Father: "Let's see . . . it's Shannon's turn to pick the activity. What would you like to do from the list of activities that would take about 30 to 45 minutes?" (Taking turns and practical pre-planning)

Shannon: "How about playing badminton in the back yard and having cookies and lemonade following the game?"

Scott: "Great. I'm good at badminton! What kind of cookies? Chocolate chip?"

Mother: "Fine. It's settled then. I'll mark the calendar." (Pre-planning)

Individual Activities

Use the FFA list for ideas on individual activities that would be appropriate for your child. Also, be attentive to the activities in which she excels or wishes to do well.

Guide her choice of activities toward those in which her friends will want to get—and can get—involved. Other sources of ideas for individual activities are your local YMCA/ YWCA, parks and clubs, governmentally organized activities, and after-hours school activities. Examples: exercise or dance class, bowling league, gymnastics, music lessons, karate, Scouts, a religious youth group, a school club, a sports league.

This should be mandatory for each family member too. Some children are satisfied never leaving the TV—this should not be allowed. Nor should the parent pressure or allow the child to get involved in so many activities that the child has insufficient time for rest, study, family responsibilities, and unstructured leisure time.

Again, try to keep the cost low. If heavy expenditures are involved for membership fees, uniforms, equipment, commuting, and so forth, the parents should get a commitment from the child that she will participate in the activity for an appropriate length of time or for the duration of the event or league.

The steps of organizing the child's individual activities are similar to organizing the family activities: You explore the possibilities for enjoyment; then you plan and execute them.

First you can check the family list for activities the child specifically mentioned enjoying. Then you can add to that list by exploring what's available nearby and within your price range. Lastly, you can sit down with the child and ask for her ideas. Then ask whether she would enjoy any listed activities that she didn't mention.

Once you have helped the child settle on as many activities as he can fit reasonably into his schedule, you can sign him up for the activities. Watch overscheduling though! A child with a different place to go nearly every day after school has no time for family (much less homework). And an overscheduled child becomes "average" at a lot of things but "expert" at nothing, since there is no time to concentrate on and practice anything! As a general guide, elementary-age children probably need no more than a once-a-week activity. Most teens cannot handle more than two weekly activities if they are to give quality time to their schoolwork, family, and themselves. I hear too many parents complain that they spend more time with their child in the car, "hauling" the child to the next activity, than anyplace else! This is unhealthy—as well as exhausting—and on the way to developing more stressed-out Type A personalities.

You can help your child with any advance preparation required, such as equipment, fees, and so forth. You can mark your calendar with the dates and times and arrange for any needed transportation. You child is on his way to the time of his life, and a happier childhood.

REINFORCING TECHNIQUE 4:
Influencing the Child's Choice of Friends

Many parents fantasize about finding a way to guide their child toward making constructive friendships. It often remains a dream though, because children usually resent and resist parental influence over their choice of friends. Often a parent has only to comment unfavorably about a friend for the child to immediately seek out that friend before others.

The choice of her friends is one of the child's most important concerns at the moment *and* an opportunity to practice and establish her ability to make judgments, which assures others of her independence.

Despite the obstacles, parents *can* reach their children and provide effective guidance, influencing a child's selection of friends and reducing negative peer pressure without raising suspicions that they are interfering in their child's social life.

Your first step is to become more aware of exactly who the members of your child's peer group are, as well as what type of behavior they cultivate and what their interests are.

Exactly how does this knowledge of your child's peer group help you influence your child's choice of friends? When you see a peer you have identified as trouble appear on the horizon, your "alarm" goes off and you take action whenever you can.

Your second step is to redirect the child, and there are two strategic actions to this step. One is distraction: you refocus the child's attention, distracting her from "trouble" peers by offering *other activities;* and you'll be able to see, from the FFA list you've developed, what kinds of activities will appeal to the child. You'll also know better when to use distraction to discourage further association with problem peers and to encourage friendships with *other, more wholesome peers.* Of course, if a peer is serious trouble, you may have to forbid your child to continue the association.

This is the easiest way to begin influencing your child's choice of friends. As your understanding of your child's environment and her reactions to it improves, you may want to put into action the second strategy for influencing your child's choice of friends.

The second strategic action is discussion: you and your child talk about the issue of friendship, or any related issues, in order to increase the child's objectivity about her peers.

In essence, you are asking the child to give her opinion about something, a request which children find just as flattering as adults do. You are encouraging her openness to discussion by approaching her on an "adult" level, by showing interest, and by approving of her participation in the discussion. At the same time, you are improving your understanding of, and communication with, your child.

You are not offering *your* opinion of her less-than-optimal friendships—an opinion that would likely include some criticism. With this method of discussion, you are relieved of that finger-pointing burden, which would result in loss of control over your child and in loss of your child's trust in you.

This second approach—of teaching your child to choose friends wisely—is a sensitive one; and we'll discuss more about how to handle it delicately later in this section, after you have absorbed the concept of the influencing technique of distraction.

Guidelines follow to help you put into action the two steps to influencing your child's choice of friends:

1. **Get to know the child's circle of friends.**

2. **Redirect the child: Use distraction and discussion to influence the child's choice of friends and activities.**

Influencing Step 1: Get to Know the Child's Circle of Friends

Clearly, you need to know exactly who is included in the child's circle of friends, as well as what kind of behavior they cultivate and what their interests are, before you can influence the child's peer choices. You may believe you already know who the list will include and all about them; and it may turn out that, in fact, you do. Or the following two strategies may help you turn up a few names or interests you overlooked.

Your first strategic action is to make a *complete* list, so that you're better prepared to take action. You want to use the information to prevent your child from spending a lot of time with troublesome friends.

In addition to making a complete list, you should meet the child's friends in your own home. Once you have seen them in more than a superficial setting, you will be able to draw more accurate conclusions about the type of list you're holding. You will be able to decide where your influence should be focused in order to help reduce the impact of negative peer pressure within the child's peer group.

So the two strategic actions for getting to know the child's circle of friends are

- **Make a list for yourself of the child's friends.**
- **Meet the friends by having them visit the child in your home.**

Make a List of the Child's Friends

For the best results, start this list as soon as the child begins making friends, and maintain it faithfully over time. Of course, it's never too late to start. But it may take many days of communicating with your child before you can complete it.

Include in this list the ages, phone numbers, addresses, and interests of the children, as well as the names of their parents.

Then listen to your child. Listen casually for new names that come up in her conversations with you or others. Also add to the list those children who telephone, stop by to visit, are in a car pool, stop by to pick up your children for activities, are at the school bus stop, and so forth.

Listen to your child to find out whether the peers she's choosing are merely convenient or the type of friends she'd choose freely under any circumstance.

It's effective, when collecting data, to be casual. Talking with your child about activities she has or has not enjoyed each day naturally touches on the peers with whom she's spending time.

Meet the Child's Friends in Your Home

The second action strategy for getting well acquainted with your child's peer group is to have his friends visit in your home. As mentioned, having the opportunity to be around them for more than a brief meeting will help you know more about them. Watch and listen to their behavior toward you, as well as toward your child and others, as they're interacting in a natural way. This will help you identify behavior patterns and interests that characterize your child's peer group.

A side benefit of this plan is that you are encouraging your child and his friends to think of your home as a place to have fun. This is not only a healthy development; it also enables you to supervise and subtly direct free-time activities.

Plan with the child some at-home activities that include different friends, preferably one peer at a time. You will want to spend a little time with each friend to get better acquainted. Parents often get off to a smoother start with the socializing if they have their child invite a small group of friends over to the house before inviting each friend, from the small group and larger circle of friends, over to the house individually.

In advance, the parent should establish a place in the house where the child and his friend will have some degree of privacy—such as the child's room (no teen boy/girl visitations in the bedroom), the den, the back porch—so that he will want to continue with the visits all the way through the list of friends. Parents are wise who keep the house reasonably tidy, so the child is not embarrassed to invite friends over.

Plan in advance with the child what light snacks you'll offer. Your child will enjoy and look forward to the visits with more excitement if he participates. And he'll be learning gracious hospitality at the same time.

Whether the visit is individual or group in nature, you can occasionally step in and out throughout the duration of the visit. This provides an opportunity to observe the children without being a nuisance, which might discourage your child from arranging future visits. This also lets the peers know that the child has an actively interested parent.

Eventually, as the child's friendships develop, you should plan to meet the *parents* of each friend. This is especially important to do as your child matures and is out of the home more often and under others' supervision. Also, when your child will be visiting another's home, you should speak with the parents to be sure that the child will be suitably chaperoned. Questions to ask include "Are you going to be home the entire time my child is visiting?" and "Do you allow them to leave and go other places?"

If your teen is attending a party, then you need to ask the parents not only if they will be home, but also "Will you be visible during the party?"; "Will alcohol be allowed?"; and "Can kids come in and out of the party at will?" Don't assume that you know the answers to these questions because you "know" the other child's parents. I've seen disasters occur because a child's parents failed to "check out" parties! Realize that there are parents who will provide alcohol to your child under the guise of "teaching responsible drinking." What message are we sending to young people when we encourage breaking the law? In addition, alcohol consumption by youngsters will increase, because they will drink *with* adults as well as away from them.

For both the get-acquainted visits by peers to your home and your child's outings, it's a good idea to participate by bringing food, providing transportation, helping to chaperon, or joining your child afterward to help clean up. This provides you more get-acquainted time with peers and their parents, and it helps them learn about you. It's a good message to all that you are a caring, concerned, and active parent.

Influencing Step 2: Redirect the Child

Now that you are well acquainted with your child's friends and know what they like to do with their time, you may have concerns about some of those friends and the kind of negative peer pressure they exert. Perhaps they are actively pressuring your child to participate in troublesome activities, or you strongly suspect that, given the chance, they would do so. In either case, you need to take Influencing Step 2, **Redirect the Child.**

As we saw earlier, the two strategic actions you can take to redirect your child are distraction and discussion:

- **Distract the child's attention and divert her energies toward different, healthier, interesting activities, and the peers with whom to enjoy them.**

- **Discuss the art of choosing good friends and establishing constructive friendships.**

Distract the Child

When you see that the child is spending or planning to spend a significant amount of time with peers who generate negative pressure, you will want to try to break that up a little. You don't want what you're doing to be obvious. You can distract her in a positive, unobtrusive way—one that will keep the child happy—by redirecting her to other activities and peers.

If the child has already made plans with a problem peer, tell her that you are in the mood for a fun activity that just happens to conflict with her plans. Always select an activity that you know the child will *prefer*, so that she will be eager to change her plans and will feel that she herself has chosen in favor of the activity with you. Let *her* make the suggestion that she cancel her other plans; just make sure that, to be polite, she gives the peer sufficient advance notice. Your position is "It's up to you," and you maintain that position throughout the discussion, holding your breath and hoping that she chooses the activity you've proposed. If the attempt doesn't work, and she keeps her original plans, you can try again soon for better success.

If the child has free time coming up and no plans for it, and you fear that she'll make plans with a troublesome peer, don't wait for a problem to develop—immediately do some planning with the child yourself. Get her mind off the problem peer by including new peers in the activity, or good friends whom she doesn't get to see very often after school, such as schoolmates who live at a distance. Literally go the "extra mile" to provide transportation for those other, more positive children. You'll often find that the parents of the other children are more than willing to meet you and *your* offspring halfway, for reasons similar to yours!

You can also keep the child busy with sports, extracurricular lessons, pets, hobbies, chores, earning extra "fun" money, and so forth. Remember that the child with a structured life is less apt to be bored and spends most of her time constructively, with similarly motivated peers.

The Problem Peer

Suppose you have serious concerns about a peer with whom your child regularly gets into serious trouble. You have decided that they consistently make poor decisions together.

Allowing the friends to continue to spend free time together is very risky for your child. The only 100 percent effective way to ensure that your child is no longer pressured into trouble by the peer, or that the peer is no longer pressured by your child, is to forbid their association out of school. If you use the discussion technique demonstrated next, you can help the child understand your decision, and you can suggest that they don't associate during school time, either. Whether or not you discuss it, your decision should be final and not open to debate!

You may take the risk of allowing their continuing association because you feel sorry for the troublesome peer. That peer may have many problems, such as parents who fight, the appearance of not being well cared for, a cruel parent, and so forth. You naturally feel compassion for the child. The risk is when you allow or encourage your child to try to help that peer out of his difficulties.

When a child is a drug user, a school truant, a runaway, or in other serious trouble, he needs adult help. Your child cannot "save" him by associating with him or trying to provide him with a good example. The danger to which you are exposing your child is that of the peer negatively influencing your child.

Unfortunately, the negative result is more common. The odds are against your child being able to help the peer and in favor of injury to your child. You certainly don't want to play those odds. You are perfectly within your rights and responsibilities as a parent to curtail this negative association.

So try to avoid feeling guilty about the other child when you refuse to let your child associate with him. You owe it to your child. If you want to take an active role in helping the troubled peer, try using the techniques in the "Multi-Parental Networking" section of this guidebook. Or, if the situation is really serious, you can contact the appropriate authorities or agencies, such as school counselors, social services, and so on.

How do you discuss your decision to remove your child from an endangering influence?

Express your concern about the effect the peer and your child are having on each other. Your child needs to see that you are concerned about *him*. It is also important that you mention your generic complaint(s), so that your child will see why you are concerned and understand that you have not taken an irrational dislike to the peer.

An example of a generic complaint is, "When you and Bruce get together, you too often go somewhere you aren't allowed to go. We are sorry to say that he is an unacceptable friend for you, and we want you to choose someone else to (do such and such) with."

Avoid mentioning specific instances of past troubles with the peer, as the child can use this to lead you into debating your decision.

Discuss the Art of Choosing Good Friends

Discussion of good friends is best suited for either the younger, more receptive child, or the older child with whom you have a relationship that is understanding, nonjudgmental, and very open in communication.

If you feel that is not true for your child or your relationship at this stage, you can fall back solely on the distraction action for now. The longer you use that parenting technique, along with the other skills in this book, the more adjusted your child will become to healthy activities and behavior, and the more receptive she will be to discussion later.

The distraction technique is a natural before-the-discussion technique with most children, unless the child is highly self-motivated to choose friends well. Then you can bypass distraction. Once you have had this discussion, going back to distraction is less effective, since the child is then aware of your goals in regard to her peers. That is fine, because discussion is a step beyond distraction. Distraction is the *parent* in action; after discussion, the *child* takes the PPR action.

The goals of this strategic action are as follows:

- To discuss qualities found in good friends

- To help the child evaluate objectively the character of her friends

This action is a sensitive one and must be handled delicately to avoid upsetting and alienating the child, who may feel her independence is threatened.

The only reason this discussion approach can work with a normally sensitive child is that the technique involves asking the child's opinion and offers your flattering, uncritical attention to her ideas. Children are no different from adults in enjoying someone's interest in their thoughts. When handled well, this technique approaches the child on an adult level, which is flattering to her.

You are not offering *your* opinion, which, in the interest of improvement, is bound to contain criticism. Criticism often closes the door on this discussion for a long, long time.

This discussion should be informal and relaxed. This is not school or an interview, but rather a "chit-chat." Try not to make it obvious that you are holding a parent-to-child communication, but rather conduct it as a chat stimulated by your friendly curiosity and interest. Do not appear disappointed in your child at any time during the conversation. You're not there to judge; you're there to listen and to guide. Be charming, and as always, be positive.

Suggestions follow to effectively redirect the child's choice of friends through discussion.

First, ask the child what qualities she finds in good friends. Asked in such a way, the child infers that you believe she has used mature judgment so far in acquiring friends. So you're starting on an inspiring, nonthreatening, trust-building tone.

Continue by letting the child take time to think of a good list. Letting the child generate the ideas and draw the conclusions is an actual learning step. Your guidance after she finishes is merely reinforcement and extra suggestion. Primarily, she will act later on ideas she thought of herself.

Look involved, nod, and verbally agree with the ideas the child lists, unless they are obviously erroneous. Then mentally review her list and see if she has left out anything important.

If the child does not mention any of the following qualities, you should suggest them. Phrase those suggestions as questions so that she will have to continue thinking on her own.

Some qualities to look for in good friends:

— Obeys parents

— Follows rules and laws

— Does well in school

— Has positive attitude

— Is thoughtful of others' well-being

— Is involved in fun, constructive activities

— Does not use tobacco, alcohol, or other drugs

If it becomes obvious that she is not going to think of one or more of these qualities, then ask, "What about _____?" and let her discuss what she understands that quality to involve. Don't prompt her. Then ask in the same way about the next quality she missed.

Next, help the child evaluate his friends. This may be the first time the child has ever been taught to deliberately, rationally, and objectively evaluate his friendships.

Some of the friends may be in his peer group simply because they're neighbors, or they ride the same bus, or they're in the same class, or they've known each other forever, or they're relatives. Some of those peers may not have qualities the child would have chosen in his friends.

He may have been going along unthinkingly with the trouble-making suggestions of those peers. If he evaluates the peers objectively, he may do better in the future with regard to saying no or seeking out other friends.

When you ask the child to evaluate his friends, do it in the context of your discussion. Remember that evaluation naturally follows definition: *After* the child has thought about what makes a good friend, it's only natural, and logical, for him to consider specifically which of his friends "fit the bill."

As you suggest that he evaluate his friends, gently lead him to consider each of them in light of the qualities he just outlined. You probably cannot expect him to confide to you all of his newly forming opinions of the friends. Your uncritical guidance and attention, however, are necessary to get him thinking about the positive and negative attitudes of the people he has chosen to be his friends.

Your aim is to help him think about his associates and draw his own conclusions about which are good company and which he should spend less time with from now on.

Mention that he may want to consider the peers who he has decided are trouble and to think about what good qualities they are missing—what has put them on his list of trouble friends instead of good friends. Allowing him to do his own thinking is far more effective than imposing your opinions on him.

Ask him which of the 10 PPR responses he feels will work with those trouble peers when they pressure him.

Through this gentle process, you will help your child to look objectively at his friends' characters, decide what he thinks about each one, and be better prepared for future interaction with them. Hopefully, you will see a shift toward his spending more time with the friends he has judged to be positive, and less time with the others. Additionally, he is now better equipped to make good choices when making new friends in the future.

Influencing: Wrap-Up

You have now made a list for yourself of the child's peers. You have gotten to know them from visits to your home. They now are enjoying socializing in your home more, and are out "roaming" less. Your child feels you are showing a genuine, flattering interest in his social development and recreation.

Also, your child has a better understanding of his friends and what to expect from them. He knows more about choosing wisely whom he will spend his time with and what kind of new friends he wants to attract. He knows which peers are definitely off-limits after school hours, if any. He's more conscious, too, of the qualities that will make him a desirable friend to others, and his friendships should gradually become healthier.

These are such desirable conditions that you naturally want to sustain them. Simply recycle the two steps of this parenting technique by doing the following:

- Regularly update your FFA list and list of peers.

- Meet any new additions to the list of peers.

- Quietly monitor on an ongoing basis the balance of time your child spends with different friends.

When you hear a new name or activity come up, add it to your list. Also, update your list periodically by deleting the names of peers your child has "dropped." This can be an encouraging barometer of your child's growing success. And as you meet his new friends, it can help you monitor any problems and stop them before they get started.

Isn't it a good feeling to know that you don't have to be helpless about dealing with the influence peers have on your child?

REINFORCING TECHNIQUE 5:
Taking Advantage of Multi-Parental Networking

You are not alone! There are other parents interested in reversing the increasingly negative peer pressures in the lives of today's youth.

The parents of the children in a peer group can organize or improve a communication network, which will identify common areas of parental concern and ways to improve those trouble areas. Then you can cooperate as a unified group (or like an "extended family") to help reduce the negative pressure that is currently built into the structure of the peer group.

Such a unit of parents can also give you emotional and advisory support in your individual PPR efforts with your child. Sharing can help each parent feel less overwhelmed and alienated. Not only can it improve your attitude, it can provide you with information about the child and the peers, and help alert you to problems about which you should know.

Other parents, including your spouse, can be good resources for several reasons. They have different parenting experiences, which can stimulate learning, as well as different perspectives from which you can gain a more complete, conscious picture of your child's peer-group environment.

Parents can also act as an extended family and, when you're not there but they are, can reinforce the skills of responsibility that you're teaching your child.

Other parents can also foster that responsible behavior in *their* children. Thus, your child and theirs are confronted with fewer, less-intense occasions of the kind of trouble from which they must rescue themselves with PPR, or from which they must be distracted.

Lastly, parents can be sources of education on new information.

The primary focus of the multi-parent group is on positively shaping and controlling the environment of the children's peer group, and creating an atmosphere more conducive to the skills of PPR. The secondary focus is to support the individual parent. The aim is not just to reduce negative pressure but also to encourage positive behavior in the group.

People tend to go along with the status quo, and children are no exception. Perhaps even more than adults, they tend to confirm the status quo rather than act individually. Therefore, when their friends have similar rules and expectations at home, it is easier for all of them to act responsibly.

The results of taking advantage of the network possibilities for parents are successful, which is evidenced by the growing number of groups for parents in this country. Parents across the nation are organizing these communication/support associations to create healthier environments for their children.

Now that you're inspired to join forces with those other parents out there, let's talk practically about the specifics of organizing.

Talk Is Cheap But Can Be Valuable

The parents in a group may plan to benefit from any or all of the following possible results.

The first accomplishment of a support group grows out of talking on the phone or (preferably) meeting one another to get acquainted. It results in open dialogue and the improvement of communication among the parents of children in a peer group.

In addition to adding to your knowledge of your child's world, such dialogue can help you discover the expectations of other parents for their children. Thus, you will have a better understanding of what pressures your child experiences in the peer group. You will also improve your communication with your child as a positive side effect.

In addition to the expectations of other parents, you will identify common areas of concern for the children. You may be alerted to some of which you were not aware, and agree on others about which you have been concerned or undecided.

Discussion of others' successes and failures can also stimulate new parenting ideas and help you practice prevention by learning from others' mistakes.

Getting better acquainted with the parents will show you how much you can rely on them for support of your standards when they are responsible for your child. You can all act for each other as a monitoring, extended family. You will also discover to what degree they practice your type of guidance and control.

Once you have made such a discovery, open dialogue can give you an opportunity to suggest consistent, group-wide rules and activities for the children. Consistent behavior guidelines can be developed and enforced by united parents.

Parents can be sources of information about mutual concerns by sharing news, professional advice, and other kinds of informative materials they have picked up. You can expand your information beyond what you have time to collect for yourself. You and others can work together to acquire new information and to educate yourselves on issues of concern facing your children in this society.

A burden shared is a lighter burden. When parents share their parenting experiences and concerns, they develop team spirit, which makes the load seem lighter because they have advice, emotional support, and other kinds of help available to them. And just knowing that others are experiencing similar problems helps you put yours in perspective. You realize that your concerns are not necessarily out of proportion to those of the rest of the world. Your attitude and optimism can get a real boost.

In addition to improving communication and understanding among all involved, steps are being taken toward constructive action, consistent rules, and healthy activities, group-wide.

When?

The support group should be started (or joined, if one already exists) as soon as your child begins to interact regularly with others outside the family circle and to develop her own friendship circles.

The group meets as often as necessary after the initial meeting. This can be determined by the degree of negative behavior that is exhibited by the peer group under discussion.

Where?

The group may meet informally at the home of one of the parents, or they may get together at a more public, neighborhood meeting spot, which can lend a greater sense of importance to the meetings.

The best place to hold a meeting is a location that consistently attracts the most parents, so convenience and comfort are considerations too. The group may be so informal that the parents network by phone, but the group that meets regularly in person to accomplish specific goals will accomplish more. However, the most important issue is that parents do communicate, and communicating informally is better than not at all!

No special equipment is needed beyond your basic pad and pencil. You may want to have a calendar and an address directory handy.

Who?

Before you tackle the "How" action, you must plan your "Who." Once you decide whom to contact, then you can go into action.

The possibilities for the membership list are endless. Usually the group includes the parents of a regular circle of friends and possibly peer relatives. "Regular" means children who play together or visit one another at least once a month.

The membership need not be limited to the child's closest peer friends and relatives. It may be organized with parents from the child's homeroom, classroom(s), or grade level. It may include parents of children who join with yours in organized outside activities. It may comprise the parents of the neighborhood, since children of dissimilar ages in a neighborhood often play together because they're available. Perhaps you may be a member of more than one group. You should belong to at least one group: that which includes your child's closest friends.

The factor that most strongly influences the type and size of group membership is the primary goal of the group.

For example, if the primary goal is simply to get acquainted with the parents of a large peer category, and perhaps to provide the children with group-activity alternatives, the group can be larger and more diverse.

If the major goal is to become a closely knit group attempting to significantly reduce negative pressure in a group of peers, then the numbers will be smaller since the group will necessarily be smaller. In this instance, a larger group could run into trouble when aiming for unanimous consistency.

How?

Here's a list of the simple steps for putting an active group into motion:

1. **List your child's peers and activities.**

2. **Recruit help.**

3. **Plan and prepare for the first meeting.**

4. **Hold the first meeting.**

Networking Step 1: List Your Child's Peers and Activities

You probably will have already developed this list as suggested in the previous section, "Influencing Your Child's Choice of Friends."

If you wish to broaden the group membership as just discussed, choose your category(s) and refer to any available school directories, organization lists, address books, and phone directories.

Your list will most likely be larger than your actual attendance, as there is usually a percentage of "no-shows" who miss meetings for various reasons. The more effective your group becomes, the more excitement it will generate, and attendance will therefore improve.

Networking Step 2: Recruit Help

You usually can't, and shouldn't try to, organize the group without help. Your chances of being well received are better when you have some support. You won't seem pushy or alarmist, and will appear more structured in your approach, once you've already gained some support. And your proposed membership will feel more comfortable about aligning themselves with the parent group.

Choose one parent from another family to be the co-leader. Choose an individual who is likely to be receptive and supportive of you and the group, and who will be well received by others.

You will probably find such support in the parents of your child's very best friends. If not, look to a parent in the peer group who appears to take a strong, active role in parenting.

Networking Step 3: Plan and Prepare for the First Meeting

The initiator of the program will probably host the first meeting.

— Prepare the list of parents who must be notified of the meetings, complete with phone numbers and the best times to reach them.

— Plan the date, place, time, refreshments (if any), and possible topics for discussion at the meeting. Prepare notes on what to say to parents when inviting them to attend the meeting. To motivate attendance, emphasize the purpose of the meeting.

— Be persistant: Keep calling until you have reached everyone on the list. Stress the importance of attendance. If anyone seems to need a second call as a reminder before the meeting, then provide it. And don't be discouraged by those parents who you thought really needed the group but didn't attend. That will happen to some extent in the best of networking groups, and the other parents can still achieve a positive outcome for the peer group.

Now that you've done your networking homework, you're ready to communicate.

Demonstration—Preparing for First Parent Meeting

Leader:

"Hello. May I please speak with Mitzi Simmons? . . . Hello, Mrs. Simmons. My name is Kay Jackson. I'm Jeremy's mother. Our sons are in the same class at school. . . . I'm calling to invite you to the first meeting of a parent network system we are developing. We are inviting parents of our children's peer group to the meeting, to be held on October 19th at 123 Main Street. We feel that if the parents could get acquainted with each other, we could accomplish several goals, such as helping our children deal with peer pressure and encourag-

208

ing healthier activities group-wide. The meeting won't last over an hour, and we need your and your husband's presence to make the initial planning session successful."

Mrs. Simmons:

"I can come that night, but I'll have to check with my husband."

Leader:

"Great! We hope he can make it too. We'll have light refreshments at the end of the meeting, so we can have some informal 'chit-chat.' So glad you can come! . . . See you then. Goodbye."

Networking Step 4: Hold the First Meeting

Here are some agenda items that have proven successful with other groups:

— Members introduce themselves.

— A group leader is selected to moderate at the meetings. The need for a group secretary is discussed. If the group decides one is needed, there is a call for a volunteer. The secretary's job is to take notes on the meetings, to organize and update the membership list, and to distribute copies of the list and any other useful information.

— To get the group thinking in the right direction, you can distribute copies of a parent-survey form. This makes suggestions of topics and concerns. It can be used to stimulate ideas and, if desired, as a permanent list of goals. The leader can collect the forms and quickly review them for a consensus of group concerns. (A sample parent-survey form is provided at the conclusion of this section.)

— Each attendee contributes by expressing an area of concern as a parent. Examples are dating and curfew guidelines, movies and TV viewing, behavioral expectations, appropriate privileges, appropriate responsibilities, lack of appropriate activities.

Example: "What are some guidelines that we as parents should set for teenage parties in our homes?" A list of guidelines for all to follow should include these items: plan a guest list and allow no party crashers; set a definite beginning and ending time for the party; forbid the use of tobacco, alcohol, and other drugs; have more than two adults supervise larger parties; allow lights to be dimmed but not turned off; do not let teens leave the party and later return; help your teen plan for refreshments, acceptable games and music, and so forth. Parents whose children will be attending a party should feel comfortable calling the host parents to ensure that these guidelines are going to be met.

— Led by the leader, develop a list of group goals that are practical and reasonably achievable, based on the concerns expressed. If the group decides to modify child behavior group-wide, additional discussion may be required before guidelines can be developed and adopted by all. A second meeting may be helpful, providing members with time to think and observe. Or the leader may feel that the discussion should be completed at the first meeting so that momentum is not lost.

— Collect any missing parent data (phone numbers, etc.).

— Set next group-meeting date, place, and time before adjourning meeting.

— Organize any necessary efforts to acquire educational materials or to conduct other behind-the-scenes work.

Demonstration—
Parent-Survey Form: Meeting Topics

PARENT-SURVEY FORM: MEETING TOPICS

1. How can we reduce harmful peer pressure in the group?

   For example:

   — smoking   — dangerous driving

   — mature movies   — vandalism

   — drinking/other   — clothing-brand
     drug use   pressures

   — unsupervised   — sneaking out
     parties   of the house

   _____

   _____

   _____

2. How can we encourage the development of a more positive self-image in our children?

   _____

   _____

   _____

3. How can we establish any needed babysitting, co-opting, after-school-care, and social-chaperoning systems?

   _____

   _____

   _____

(continued)

PARENT-SURVEY FORM: MEETING TOPICS
(continued)

4. Do we need to evaluate activities affecting our children's values and behavior? If so, which ones?

For example:
- movies
- rock concerts
- TV shows
- music
- community and peer recreational activities

_____

_____

_____

_____

5. Do we need more parent education on any of the following?
(Check one or more boxes.)

❏ substance use

❏ effective parenting

❏ allowances

❏ nutrition

❏ neighborhood and school safety

❏ supervision of teenage parties

❏ other:

❏ peer pressure

❏ disciplining

❏ children's rewards

❏ children's privileges

❏ pool, water, and summer safety

❏ household responsibilities

_____

_____

PARENT-SURVEY FORM: MEETING TOPICS
(continued)

6. How does our adult behavior sometimes send the wrong messages to children, and thus encourage harmful behavior?

For example:

—"I can't start the day without my cup of coffee."

—"I can't sleep without my *xyz* pills" (or "lose weight" or "deal with *xyz* problems").

—"I've had a rough day at the office. I think I need a beer" (or "cocktail," etc.).

— Leaving adult books and magazines lying around; watching adult TV and movies; watching TV and movies all the time; playing music that depicts immoral sex and violence, or that glorifies those who do.

— Mentioning with interest, perhaps even approval, celebrities or acquaintances who represent poor values or superficial attributes.

— Using a radar detector.

_____

_____

_____

7. Your further suggestions for meeting topics:

_____

_____

_____

_____

(continued)

PARENT-SURVEY FORM: MEETING TOPICS
(concluded)

8. Other concerns:

_____

_____

_____

_____

Thanks! We're now on the road to holding constructive meetings—ones that will benefit all of us and our children!

Construct your own parent survey for the meeting if you need different or additional questions for your particular situation.

Avoid getting "bogged down" in unproductive discussions about issues such as "Why are the parents who really need to be here not here?" You'll only waste time if you spend it placing blame on others for the current peer group's condition. Avoid attempting to force parents to follow the group's guidelines. Avoid bringing up actual situations that could embarrass a parent and that would be more appropriately discussed in private. Keep the problem references general to the group.

Keep your parent list up to date for future meetings. The leader and co-leader will use it to notify (and remind if necessary) parents of the next meeting, especially those who weren't at the previous meeting. The leaders should plan the agenda items as far in advance as possible and check that any needed work is done in advance. Leadership should be changed as needed so that no one gets "burned out."

SPECIAL NOTE ABOUT DRUGS

Your child may be exposed to pressure to use illegal and harmful substances, especially between the sixth and tenth grades. Unfortunately, drug use is once again on the increase among adolescents. If your child has a "romance" with, or is best friends with, a drug-using child, the chances of her also doing drugs are very strong. Fred Beauvais, a Colorado State University psychologist, found friends' habits have at least five times more impact on teen drug use than any other lifestyle factors.

If your child is using alcohol or other drugs, she may be so disoriented that she does not respond well even to the effective parenting techniques in this book. If you have any reason to suspect substance use, you should look into it further and get professional help for your child, so that you *can* reach her with your parenting skills.

Educational materials are available. If your suspicions of drug use are strong, you can have a medical doctor do a drug screen on your child for the presence of any number of drugs. This is a simple, painless procedure, whereby a urine sample from your child is analyzed. If use is confirmed, you will want to get professional help in diagnosing the problem and realigning the child toward health. Realize that if you confront your child with your suspicions, almost every drug-using youth will deny such usage. And if the child does admit to usage and promises never to do it again, the likelihood of repeat usage is *extremely* high!

There is usually a lag time of six months to a year before parents recognize symptoms. On the next pages you will see symptoms often associated with drug use. One list details physical symptoms; the other outlines social and emotional changes that may occur.

No *one* symptom on these lists is going to alarm a parent. However, some symptoms appear only during the "high," and few children are careless enough to come home high.

So the child may have symptoms that you are unable to see. If you do observe some of these symptoms in your child, you should be concerned in proportion to the number and seriousness of the symptoms observed.

If many symptoms appear, be careful to avoid rationalizing that your child *could not* have a drug problem because she goes to a good school, or she is monitored too closely, or she knows right from wrong. It happens all the time in the "good" families as well as the "problem" families. In fact, contrary to popular thinking, consumption of marijuana is highest among white children of highly educated, affluent suburbanites. Also keep in mind that many children use drugs just before or after school, so fewer clues are seen by parents or teachers.

At the end of the guidebook is a list of resources that can provide you with additional information on this subject.

Physical Symptoms Common to Drug Users

1. **Changes in Activity Level**
   - Fatigue, lethargy, or sleepiness
   - Periods of hyperactivity

2. **Changes in Food Consumption**
   - Appetite decrease or increase
   - Cravings for certain foods
   - Weight decrease or increase

3. **Uncoordination**
   - Staggering gait, falling, clumsiness, dropping objects
   - Slow movements or reactions

4. **Speech Patterns**
   - Slurred or garbled speech
   - Flat or expressionless speech
   - Speech that seems forced, difficult
   - Forgetting thoughts or ideas
   - Incomplete sentences

5. **Breath**
   - Shortness of breath, hacking cough
   - Peculiar odor to breath and/or clothes (marijuana)

6. **Eyes**
   - Reddened
   - Watery
   - Eyelids droopy

7. **Increased Susceptibility**
   - Colds
   - Infections
   - Runny nose

8. **Changes in Sleeping Habits**
   - Staying up all night, sleeping all day

9. **Changes in Appearance**
   - Marked change in style or color of clothes
   - Reduced interest in appearance
   - Sloppy or unkempt appearance

10. **Other Physical Symptoms**
    - Paling of normally pink-cheeked complexion
    - Tremors or shaking
    - Nausea or vomiting
    - Sweating or chills

11. **Other Mental Symptoms**
    - Lack of concentration
    - Severe nervousness, agitation, irritability
    - Short amounts of time feeling longer, or the reverse

Social and Emotional Changes Common to Drug Users

1. **Mood Alteration**
    - Changes or swings in mood: from overly happy or gregarious mood to irritability, anxiety, violence, bizarreness, depression, or outbursts of anger

2. **Thoughts**
    - Lack of thoughts; vacantness
    - Strange and bizarre thoughts
    - Hallucinations
    - Suspiciousness, even paranoid delusions
    - Depressed thoughts
    - Suicidal thoughts

3. **Withdrawal**
    - Secretiveness
    - Deviousness
    - Vagueness
    - Hypersensitivity
    - Placing his/her room "off limits" to family

4. **Sudden Switches in Friendships**
    - Disdain for old friends
    - New acquaintances phoning
    - Frequenting of new hang-outs
    - Acquaintances stopping by for very short periods of time

5. **Performance**
   - Drop in school participation/grades
   - School truancy
   - Resentment toward teachers
   - Avoiding school work
   - Lack of interest and concentration span in school, hobbies, or anything
   - Amotivational ("I don't care") syndrome

6. **New Idols**
   - Older kids
   - Strong pull toward drug-using rock stars, or songs with drug lyrics

7. **Legal Problems**
   - Keeping late hours
   - Traffic violations
   - Assaultiveness
   - Disrespect for police
   - Possession of drug paraphernalia and drugs

8. **Authority Rebellion**
   - Resentment and unreasonableness toward any authority
   - Flagrant disregard for rules—school, home, legal

9. **Paraphernalia**
   - Frequenting of paraphernalia shops and/or music shops selling paraphernalia
   - Presence of drug paraphernalia—such as incense, room deodorizers, eyedrop bottles, seeds and leaves, cigarette papers, and pill bottles—in bedroom, clothing pockets, or purse

6. PEER PRESSURE REVERSAL:

Summary

Don't you feel light-years ahead now in preparing a child for negative peer pressure? And PPR makes such practical, good sense.

With PPR, not only are you better equipped to raise a responsible child and enjoy the relationship, but you also have a tool for sharing those skills with other parents. How gratifying to enjoy the pleasing results as other children around your healthier child become more responsible and happier too.

Let's review what you've gained since you began implementing the skills in this book.

You've discovered the art of reversing peer pressure in many varieties (and even may be tempted to try some of them for yourself!). You've trained your child to **Check Out the Scene** regularly by noticing and identifying potential trouble. You've helped the child to **Make Good Decisions** by understanding and choosing consequences. And you've given your child creative, realistic responses in order to **Act to Avoid Trouble**. Your child is on the road to developing maturity and being a winner!

The results of these newly acquired skills are exciting, and they won't disappear just as you're beginning to enjoy them, because you've learned techniques for the maintenance and reinforcement of the PPR skill.

You're organized with the five teaching steps of (1) **Scheduling** a learning session, (2) **Introducing** the PPR concept, (3) **Discussing** the actual steps of the PPR skill, (4) using **Practice** to make effective PPR behavior, and (5) following through and providing **Feedback** to your child on his or her accomplishment of PPR behavior.

You're continuing to reinforce responsible behavior balanced with an enjoyable lifestyle by providing ongoing praise—**Encouraging the Positive**—and **Disciplining Effectively** when necessary to maintain your child's awareness of consequences.

Your praise and encouragement are setting a positive tone in both your child's life and the family's life together. Your consistent, fair discipline ensures that your child doesn't backslide and lose any of the strength that has been gained by learning PPR.

Now that your child's growing to be such a great kid, your natural inclination is to spend more time together! **Organized Family Activity** lets you do just that, while organized individual activities boost your child's confidence and strengthen positive self-image.

While you're at it, why not use those activities to distract your child from negative involvements and **Influence the Child's Choice of Friends**? And as the world is looking bright for both your child and your relationship, you are better able to communicate in order to help your child be objective and choose healthy friends.

Last in this increase of effective parenting is your taking advantage of "people-power"—**Taking Advantage of Multi-Parenting Networking**—by drawing other parents together for mutual support and to promote healthy behavior in their children. Rather than taking a lone stand against a world of negative pressures, you and other parents can join forces and succeed together.

Resources

For more information on drug prevention and parent/peer group networking, contact the following organizations:

- **PRIDE International, Inc.** (Parents' Resource Institute for Drug Education)
  3610 DeKalb Technology Parkway
  Suite 105
  Atlanta, GA 30340
  Phone: 770-458-9900

- **PRIDE CANADA, Inc.**
  College of Pharmacy and Nutrition
  110 Science Place
  University of Saskatchewan
  Saskatoon, Saskatchewan S7N5CN
  Canada
  Phone: 1-800-667-3747 (within Canada)

- **National Family Partnership**
  11159-B South Towne Square
  St. Louis, MO 63123
  Phone: 314-845-1933

- ***Listen Magazine*** (for teens by subscription)
  The Health Connection
  55 W. Oakridge Drive
  Hagerstown, MD 21740
  Phone: 1-800-548-8700

- **U.S. Department of Education**
  Growing Up Drug Free—A Parent's Guide to Prevention (free handbook)
  Washington, DC 20202
  Phone: 1-800-572-5580

- **Committees of Correspondence**
  24 Adams Street
  Danvers, MA 01923
  Phone: 508-774-5626

- **MADD** (Mothers Against Drunk Driving)
  511 E. John Carpenter Freeway, Suite 700
  Irving, TX 75062
  Phone: 214-744-6233

- **U.S. Department of Education**
  What Works: Schools Without Drugs
  (free handbook)
  Washington, DC 20202
  Phone: 1-800-624-0100

For further sources, contact your county and state's alcohol-abuse and other drug-abuse agencies.

OTHER BOOKS BY SHARON SCOTT

Sharon Scott's books are excellent resources for educators, youth leaders, concerned parents, teens, and children. The following titles are now available:

How to Say No and Keep Your Friends, Second Edition
(grades 5–12)

/ paperback / 173 pages
Order Code...HSNK2

Set of 18 Teaching Transparencies /
Order Code...HSNKT2

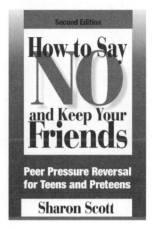

Positive Peer Groups
(for adults)

paperback / 96 pages
Order Code...PPG

When to Say Yes! And Make More Friends
(grades 5–12)

/ paperback / 120 pages
Order Code...WTSY

229

The Nicholas the Cocker Spaniel Series:

Too Smart for Trouble (grades K–4)
(Also available in Spanish from the author)

▬▬▬ paperback / 112 pages / Order Code...TST
Set of 11 Teaching Transparencies / ▬▬▬
Order Code...TSTT

Not Better...Not Worse...Just Different (grades K–5)

▬▬▬ paperback / 118 pages / Order Code...NBNWD
Set of 16 Teaching Transparencies / ▬▬▬
Order Code...NBNWT

Too Cool for Drugs (grades 1–5)
(Also available in Spanish from the author)

▬▬▬ paperback / 120 pages / Order Code...TCD
Set of 17 Teaching Transparencies / ▬▬▬
Order Code...TCDT

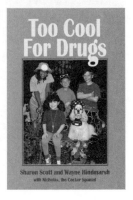

Life's Not Always Fair (grades 1–5)

▬▬▬ / paperback / 124 pages / Order Code...LNAF
Set of 17 Teaching Transparencies / ▬▬▬
Order Code...LNAFT

Also available:

- Nicholas the Cocker Spaniel (14 inch full body hand puppet)
- Teen video (Available from the author)

```
*************************************
*                                   *
*                                   *
*   WPS / Creative Therapy Store     *
*                                   *
*                                   *
*   12031 Wilshire Boulevard         *
*                                   *
*                                   *
*   Los Angeles, CA  90025-1251      *
*                                   *
*                                   *
*   (800) 648-8857                   *
*                                   *
*************************************
```

Sharon Scott as a Speaker

After reading this book, you'll probably want to hear and meet the author in person. Sharon is a convention keynote speaker, inservice consultant, and seminar leader on Peer Pressure Reversal (and 29 other topics!). Her audience includes professional helpers, parents, teens, and children.

Rather than just motivate her audience with emotional stories, she also presents proven effective skills and role-play practices to ensure her learners learn! Sharon is a versatile and dynamic speaker, well liked by both youth and adults.

Please write today for a free packet of information on her various training programs. She also provides private counseling in the North Texas area.

Sharon Scott
P.O. Box 6
Weston, Texas 75097-0006

ABOUT THE AUTHOR

Sharon Scott is a licensed professional counselor and marriage and family therapist whose internationally recognized work has been making a difference in people's lives for over 25 years. An accomplished training consultant, award-winning author, and global lecturer as well, she specializes in training programs and private counseling services. Her eight widely acclaimed books include an elementary series that she "co-authored" with her Cocker Spaniel, Nicholas.

Among Scott's many professional achievements is her Peer Pressure Reversal program—one of the most highly respected refusal programs in the nation—which she has personally brought to over one million people across the United States and in five foreign countries. She has conducted training in prevention and intervention strategies with adults and young people of all ages, from kindergarten to college. The Dallas Police Department's First Offender Program was a national model for delinquency prevention under Scott's directorship; with her assistance, police departments nationwide have created similar programs. She has received numerous honors, including the "Heart of America Award" and the 1987 and 1995 "Professional Writing Award" from the Texas Counseling Association.

A frequent TV and radio talk-show guest, Sharon Scott has appeared on *Good Morning Australia* and CNN. Hundreds of publications, including *Good Housekeeping, USA Today, Parents, Redbook, Working Mothers Magazine,* and *Teen Magazine,* have interviewed her.